Maimonides—
Essential Teachings on
Jewish Faith and Ethics

Selected Books in the
SkyLight Illuminations Series

The Art of War—Spirituality for Conflict: Annotated & Explained

Bhagavad Gita: Annotated & Explained

The Book of Job: Annotated & Explained

Chuang-tzu: The Tao of Perfect Happiness—Selections Annotated & Explained

Confucius, the Analects: The Path of the Sage—Selections Annotated & Explained

Dhammapada: Annotated & Explained

The Divine Feminine in Biblical Wisdom Literature: Selections Annotated & Explained

Ecclesiastes: Annotated & Explained

Ethics of the Sages: Pirke Avot—*Annotated & Explained*

Hasidic Tales: Annotated & Explained

The Hebrew Prophets: Selections Annotated & Explained

The Meditations of Marcus Aurelius: Selections Annotated & Explained

Native American Stories of the Sacred: Annotated & Explained

Perennial Wisdom for the Spiritually Independent: Sacred Teachings— Annotated & Explained

Proverbs: Annotated & Explained

The Qur'an and Sayings of Prophet Muhammad: Selections Annotated & Explained

Rumi and Islam: Selections from His Stories, Poems, and Discourses— Annotated & Explained

Sex Texts from the Bible: Selections Annotated & Explained

Tanya, the Masterpiece of Hasidic Wisdom: Selections Annotated & Explained

Tao Te Ching: Annotated & Explained

Zohar: Annotated & Explained

Maimonides–
Essential Teachings on
Jewish Faith and Ethics

The Book of Knowledge and the Thirteen Principles of Faith— Selections Annotated and Explained

Translation and Annotation
by Rabbi Marc D. Angel, PhD

For People of All Faiths, All Backgrounds
JEWISH LIGHTS Publishing

Walking Together, Finding the Way®
SKYLIGHT PATHS®
PUBLISHING

Maimonides—Essential Teachings on Jewish Faith and Ethics:
The Book of Knowledge and the Thirteen Principles of Faith—Selections Annotated and Explained

Translation and annotation © 2012 by Marc D. Angel

Library of Congress Cataloging-in-Publication Data
Angel, Marc.
Maimonides' essential teachings on Jewish faith and ethics : the Book of Knowledge and the Thirteen Principles of Faith : selections annotated and explained / translation and annotation by Marc D. Angel.
p. cm.
Includes the texts of Maimonides's Book of Knowledge and his Thirteen Principles of Faith in English translation.
Includes bibliographical references and index.
ISBN 978-1-59473-311-6 (quality pbk. original : alk. paper) 1. Maimonides, Moses, 1135–1204. Sefer ha-mada'. 2. Maimonides, Moses, 1135–1204. 13 'ikre ha-emunah. 3. Judaism—Doctrines. 4. Faith (Judaism) 5. Jewish ethics. I. Maimonides, Moses, 1135–1204. Sefer ha-mada'. English. II. Maimonides, Moses, 1135–1204. 13 'ikre ha-emunah. English. III. Title.
BM546.A54 2011
296.1'81—dc23

2011040592

ISBN-13: 978-1-68336-183-1 (hc)

Cover Design: Walter C. Bumford III, Stockton, Massachusetts, and Gloria Todt
Manufactured in the United States of America

SkyLight Paths Publishing is creating a place where people of different spiritual traditions come together for challenge and inspiration, a place where we can help each other understand the mystery that lies at the heart of our existence.

SkyLight Paths sees both believers and seekers as a community that increasingly transcends traditional boundaries of religion and denomination—people wanting to learn from each other, *walking together, finding the way*.®

SkyLight Paths, "Walking Together, Finding the Way" and colophon are trademarks of LongHill Partners, Inc., registered in the U.S. Patent and Trademark Office.

Published by SkyLight Paths® Publishing and Jewish Lights Publishing
An Imprint of Turner Publishing Company
4507 Charlotte Avenue, Suite 100
Nashville, TN 37209
Tel: (615) 255-2665
www.skylightpaths.com
www.jewishlights.com

In memory of my teachers,
for whom Maimonides was a living presence

Haham Dr. Solomon Gaon
Rabbi Dr. Meyer Simcha Feldblum
Rabbi Dr. Moshe Carmilly

Contents ☐

Acknowledgments   ix

Introduction   xi

Laws of Foundations of the Torah   3

Laws Relating to Moral and Ethical Character   43

Laws of Torah Study   71

Laws of Idolatry   89

Laws of Repentance   105

Thirteen Principles of Faith   151

Notes   173

Selected Bibliography   176

Acknowledgments ☐

I express my appreciation to Stuart M. Matlins, publisher of Jewish Lights and SkyLight Paths, for his role in the creation of the present volume. He suggested that I follow up on my book *Maimonides, Spinoza and Us: Toward an Intellectually Vibrant Judaism* (Jewish Lights) by preparing a translation of and commentary on Maimonides's essential teachings on Jewish faith and ethics for people of all faiths and backgrounds. I thank the Jewish Lights and SkyLight Paths staff for their excellent work in producing this volume: Emily Wichland, vice president of Editorial and Production; Heather Pelham, book design and production coordinator, who typeset this volume; and Gloria Todt, book production assistant, who contributed to the cover design. I also thank Bryna Fischer for copyediting the text and Debra Corman for her proofreading talents.

I gladly acknowledge the work of other Maimonides scholars and translators. I have learned much from them, and they have influenced my thinking in important ways. Among those who have been most helpful to my understanding of Maimonides are Marvin Fox, David Hartman Menachem Kellner, Shlomo Pines, Marc Shapiro, and Isadore Twersky. At the end of this book, I include a bibliography of their writings, as well as those of other scholars whose work has been valuable to me—and to so many other students of Maimonides.

I thank the members and supporters of the Institute for Jewish Ideas and Ideals (www.jewishideas.org), of which I am founder and director, for their unflinching commitment to an intellectually vibrant Judaism, much in the spirit of Maimonides. I thank the trustees and members of Congregation Shearith Israel, the historic Spanish and Portuguese Synagogue of New York City (founded 1654). It has been my singular privilege to serve this congregation since 1969, currently as rabbi emeritus. My Sunday morning Rambam class has been one of my ongoing joys at Shearith Israel, and I thank our class members for many lively discussions on the ideas and ideals of Maimonides.

I owe my greatest debt of gratitude to my wonderful family, each of whom is a unique treasure and source of blessing: my beloved wife, Gilda; our children, Rabbi Hayyim and Maxine Siegel Angel, Dr. Dan and Ronda Angel Arking, and Dr. James and Elana Angel Nussbaum; and our grand-children Jake Isaac Nussbaum, Andrew Zak Arking, Jonathan Marc Arking, Max Joseph Nussbaum, Charles Victor Nussbaum, Jeremy Victor Arking, Kara Lilli Nussbaum, Aviva Hayya Angel, and Dahlia Rachel Angel.

I thank the Almighty for having brought me to this special moment. I pray that this book of Maimonides's teachings on faith and ethics will be a source of strength, inspiration, and happiness to readers.

Introduction   □

Moses Maimonides (1138–1204) is one of the greatest religious thinkers of all time. In Jewish tradition, he is often called the Great Eagle, the philosopher who rose to great heights and whose vision covered an extensive range. A popular saying among Jews is that "From Moses [of the Torah] to Moses [Maimonides], none has arisen like Moses [Maimonides]." Indeed, it can fairly be asserted that from the days of Moses Maimonides until our own time, no Jewish thinker has had a more significant impact on Jewish religious thought than Maimonides.

Among his singular contributions to religious philosophy was his insistence that religion must be based on sound intellectual foundations. Since religion and reason both derive from God, it is impossible for them to be in ultimate conflict. Rather, religion and reason must exist in harmonious relationship and together must bring us closer to an understanding of God. Maimonides provided a method of mediating between revelation and reason that not only laid the groundwork for a rational, philosophically sophisticated Judaism, but provided an approach to biblical interpretation and philosophy that remains relevant for people of all faiths who follow a religion based on sacred text and oral interpretation. His approach allows a person to be religious without turning off his or her brain.

In this volume, I include a translation and commentary of Maimonides's *The Book of Knowledge* and his Thirteen Principles of Faith. These texts reflect the essential theological and philosophical teachings of Maimonides, which he presented in a lucid form intended for the widest readership. Many of the topics discussed in these works are developed in other of Maimonides's writings, notably in his major philosophical opus, *Guide of the Perplexed*. In this introduction, I will be citing passages from the *Guide* and other of his works to supplement material presented in the text of the volume itself. This will give you, the reader, a fuller perspective on the thinking of Maimonides and will enrich your understanding of the ideas presented in *The Book of Knowledge* and the Thirteen Principles of Faith.

A Medieval Jewish Philosopher: Lessons for Modern Times

Serious thinkers have pondered the state of religion in the modern period. Their discussions reflect both the turmoil and the malaise that often confront religious people of our times. American sociologist Peter Berger has written extensively about "spiritual homelessness," the breakdown in traditional faith, the feeling of deracination felt by so many moderns.[1] Well-known psychologist and Holocaust survivor Viktor Frankl has referred to the "existential vacuum" that leaves people feeling lost and spiritually empty.[2] British philosopher and historian Isaiah Berlin has lamented the growing authoritarianism and intolerance within modern religious life and has argued for a more respectful pluralism.[3] German-American Jewish social psychologist and philosopher Erich Fromm has criticized the flight from reason—on the part of some— where superstition and cults have come to replace enlightened religion.[4] Rabbi Joseph B. Soloveitchik, the most influential Orthodox Jewish thinker of the twentieth century, has characterized the dilemma of religious people in the significant title of one of his seminal lectures: "The Lonely Man of Faith."[5]

When we read of the role of religion in contemporary life, we are confronted with such topics as extremism, fanaticism, terrorism, superstition, authoritarianism, obscurantism, and hypocrisy. We are also faced with such phenomena as assimilation and secularization, and an ultraliberalism that robs religion of its core beliefs and observances.

Given the spiritual needs of our times, today's religious vision needs to be grand and compelling, intellectually rigorous and emotionally sound. It needs to rise far above popular religious discourse, which often seems parochial, sterile, and even irrational.

Moses Maimonides, the impressive thinker and teacher who lived nearly nine hundred years ago, is precisely the one who can point us in a positive spiritual direction. This medieval man was so advanced in his thinking that he is, in many respects, far more progressive than moderns. When we read his writings and contemplate his teachings, we find ourselves in the presence of one of the great religious thinkers of all time.

Maimonides's Beginnings

Moses Maimonides, popularly known in rabbinic circles by the acronym Rambam (**R**abbi **M**osheh **b**en **M**aimon), was born in Cordoba, Spain, where his father, Maimon, was a learned and respected rabbi. In 1148, Cordoba was conquered by a fanatical Muslim sect, the Almohads, who gave Jews the choice of converting to Islam or leaving the city. Thus, Maimonides's family began a period of wandering, arriving in the city of Fez in Morocco in 1160. In 1165, the family settled in Fostat, the Old City of Cairo. In 1177, Maimonides was appointed head of the Jewish community in Fostat; and in 1185, he was appointed court physician to Saladin's vizier, al-Fadil.

Given the vagaries of his life's travels and travails, it is a wonder that he had the time and mental focus to become Judaism's preeminent philosopher, Talmudic scholar, legal codifier, and spiritual leader. Maimonides's prodigious intellectual gifts were such that he was a premier rabbinic scholar and at the same time a premier philosopher and medical doctor.

Maimonides's Writings: Laying the Foundations for the Study of Jewish Ethics and Law

At age twenty-three, he began to compose a commentary on the Mishnah, the Talmudic collection of laws on all aspects of Judaism. Since the Mishnah is the foundation stone of Jewish law, Maimonides felt the need to study it thoroughly, to explain it to students of Jewish law, and to incorporate the Talmudic discussions on each passage. Through this systematic and comprehensive process, he wished to make the Mishnah accessible to students of Talmud and Jewish law. Written in Arabic and later translated into Hebrew, this commentary was completed after ten years. Aside from offering lucid explanations of the Mishnah's texts, the commentary includes three lengthy essays. In his introduction to the commentary, Maimonides discusses the nature of the Oral Torah—the body of oral tradition that accompanied the Written Torah—and the development of Jewish law, known as halakhah. The commentary also includes his introduction to chapter 10 of the tractate *Sanhedrin* (*Perek Helek*), which deals with basic principles of Jewish faith and which concludes with his Thirteen Principles of Faith. In *Shemonah Perakim* (literally, "Eight Chapters"), his introduction to the Mishnah tractate *Pirkei Avot* ("Ethics of the Fathers"), he provides a lengthy discussion of the foundations of Jewish ethics.

Upon completion of the commentary on the Mishnah, Maimonides began work on the *Mishneh Torah*, his classic code of Jewish law. This monumental project, which also took him ten years to complete, is an unparalleled achievement in the history of Jewish law. Prior to Maimonides's work, there was no systematic and comprehensive compendium of the legal rulings of the Talmud. Since the Talmudic literature is so vast, and since discussions of topics are spread throughout its many tomes, it was nearly impossible for anyone—except elite scholars—to know what the actual law required. While there were some short collections of laws composed during the few centuries before Maimonides, and while Rabbi Yitzhak Alfasi (1013–1103) had laid the foundation for the study of the legal rulings of the Talmud, there was nothing that remotely covered the entire scope of Jewish law in a clear and accessible way as did the *Mishneh Torah*. This work revolutionized the study of Jewish law. Because of its clarity and authoritative presentation, it won many advocates in the rabbinic world. On the other hand, it also met with great resistance from scholars who thought the *Mishneh Torah* would undermine the need for Talmudic study. They also resented Maimonides's arrogating to himself the right to make definitive legal rulings in all areas of halakhah. In spite of the opposition, though, the *Mishneh Torah* became a foundational classic of Jewish law, and no rabbi of subsequent generations could ignore the rulings of Maimonides.

In 1176, he began the fifteen-year labor of writing the *Guide of the Perplexed*, the single most important book of medieval Jewish philosophy. Maimonides laid the groundwork for a rational, philosophically sophisticated Judaism. Written in Arabic, it was soon translated into Hebrew and later was also translated into Latin and other European languages. Along with its powerful impact on Jewish thought, it made its mark on the thinking of such Christian philosophers and theologians as Albertus Magnus, Thomas Aquinas, and Duns Scotus.

In addition to these three major works, Maimonides also composed *The Book of Commandments*, in which he enumerated the traditional 613 commandments of the Torah, the Five Books of Moses. He wrote lengthy letters on the Jewish faith to endangered communities in Morocco and Yemen. He also wrote treatises on astrology and resurrection of the dead. Maimonides's writings include letters to individuals and communities, as well as many rabbinic responsa in which he answered halakhic questions put to him by scholars and students who sought his advice.

Additionally, Maimonides wrote copiously on scientific topics. Among these works, highly regarded in their time, are his *Treatise on Logic; Commentary on the Aphorisms of Hippocrates; Treatise on Poisons and Their Antidotes; Regimen of Health;* and *Glossary of Drug Names,* as well as others.

The Book of Knowledge: The Essential Teachings on Jewish Faith and Ethics

Maimonides opens his classic code of Jewish law, the *Mishneh Torah*, with *The Book of Knowledge. The Book of Knowledge* contains Maimonides's essential teachings on Jewish faith and ethics. Its first section is titled "Laws of Foundations of the Torah." True to his commitment to a philosophically sound religiosity, Maimonides presents basic concepts of faith that he posits must serve as the basis of proper religious life: knowledge of God, the Oneness of God, the absolute unity and incorporeality of God, the love and fear of God. He draws on the philosophical and scientific framework of ancient Greek philosophy as well as on the teachings of the Hebrew Bible and rabbinic literature.

The Book of Knowledge was sharply criticized by fundamentalist rabbis from the outset of its publication. They were troubled by Maimonides's introduction of "foreign" philosophical notions into the corpus of Jewish law and thought that the philosophical approach was dangerous to faith: it could put strange ideas into the minds of innocent students and start them on the road to intellectual speculation that could lead to heresy. As a result, these rabbis banned the study of the opening chapters of the *Mishneh Torah*. Their position was: we base our faith on the Torah and rabbinic tradition; we do not need or want to be contaminated by outside sources of wisdom, and certainly not by Greek philosophy. This anti-philosophical critique was even more sharply aimed against Maimonides's *Guide of the Perplexed*. The Jewish community was wrenched for many decades by a heated controversy between proponents and antagonists of Maimonides. Some virulent anti-Maimonideans complained to church officials in France about the "heretical" teachings of Maimonides and how his writings posed a threat to religion. This led to the 1232 public burning of copies of *Guide of the Perplexed* by Dominicans, a horrifying act that shocked even ardent anti-Maimonideans, some of whom now realized they had carried their opposition too far.

While Maimonides was certainly aware of the criticisms of his detractors, he did not back away from his position. He believed that it is imperative for religion to be based on an intellectually solid foundation, that faith without reason is highly deficient. If there is a risk to introducing philosophical concepts, there is a greater risk in not introducing them. An ignorant, unthinking faith often may encapsulate false ideas and may slip into superstition and obscurantism.

After presenting the philosophical and theological foundations of Judaism, the section on "Laws of Foundations of Torah" goes on to discuss basic topics in Jewish thought: the sanctification of God's name, the sacredness of the Hebrew Bible, the nature of prophecy, Moses as the greatest of prophets, miracles, the eternal validity of the Torah. Maimonides wants to be sure that readers have a clear and reasonable understanding of the intellectual underpinnings of Judaism.

The second section of *The Book of Knowledge* is "Laws Relating to Moral and Ethical Character." While religion requires the attainment of correct theological beliefs as explained in "Laws of Foundations of the Torah," it also entails a commitment to develop proper moral character and righteous ethical behavior. Maimonides provides guidance on how one must generally follow the "middle path," avoiding extreme dispositions. He advocates a life characterized by spiritual serenity, honesty, sincere piety, and compassion. He condemns the vices of jealousy, lust, desire for honor, greed, and similar such traits. In following the ways of God we are not confined to our moral dispositions, ethical acts, and good manners. Doing so also requires that we meet our physical needs by living a healthful lifestyle. In short, we serve God with the totality of our being.

It is interesting to note that subsequent codifiers of Jewish law—all of whom drew heavily on the work of Maimonides—seldom included these first two sections in their work. The two most significant such codes—the *Tur Shulhan Arukh* by Rabbi Jacob ben Asher (ca. 1270–1340) and the *Shulhan Arukh* by Rabbi Joseph Karo (1488–1575)—both open immediately with practical laws and rituals, that is, what to do when awakening in the morning, the blessings and prayers to be recited, and the like. Maimonides stands alone as the towering spiritual eagle who insists on setting the intellectual and moral foundations of halakhah. It is not enough to know what to do and what not to do: we first need to know why.

In the third part of *The Book of Knowledge*, "Laws of Torah Study," Maimonides underscores the centrality of Torah study as a pillar of Jewish life. Torah study leads to proper action. While Torah study is vital, Maimonides is harshly critical of those who do not engage in earning their livelihoods, but who choose rather to study Torah full-time and live off the charity of others. This is a disgrace to the Torah. The section also discusses the community's responsibility to establish schools for its children, the respect due to teachers, the teacher's obligation to respect students, and other topics relating to Torah education.

The fourth part of *The Book of Knowledge* is "Laws of Idolatry." In this section, Maimonides describes how humanity fell into the errors of idolatry and how the Jews' forefather Abraham led the way for a return to true faith in the One God. The essential commandment relating to idolatry is the prohibition to worship any created thing, but rather only to serve the One God. It is also forbidden to consult with soothsayers, sorcerers, and such; rather, a person must be pure in serving God directly.

In the fifth part of *The Book of Knowledge*, "Laws of Repentance," Maimonides outlines the emotional and behavioral patterns of repentance. When a person transgresses a ritual law—a sin between a human being and God—the person must confess the sin and resolve not to repeat it in the future. When a person sins against a fellow human being, he or she must seek atonement and gain forgiveness from the injured party—as well as repenting before God. A sin against a human being is also a sin against God. Beginning in chapter 3 of this section, Maimonides lists those sinners who lose their place in the world to come unless they undergo sincere and complete repentance. Among these sinners are those who deny basic principles of Jewish faith, as outlined in "Laws of Foundations of the Torah." Maimonides also provides a list of the kinds of sins for which atonement is very difficult, such as when a person has sinned against the public, or has spread gossip and does not know all the people it may have reached. This section includes a discussion of free will, God's love of penitents, reward and punishment, the world to come, the Messiah, and the messianic era.

The Thirteen Principles of Faith:
The Tenets of Judaism for the Masses

Maimonides included the Thirteen Principles of Faith at the conclusion of his introduction to *Perek Helek*, in his commentary on the Mishnah. In it, he discusses various themes relating to reward and punishment, messianic days, the world to come and other basic topics in Jewish faith. He composed the Thirteen Principles so that the masses of Jews would have a clear, philosophically sound formulation of the tenets of Judaism.

In the *Mishneh Torah,* he discusses each of these principles separately but does not present them as a unified list of dogmas. Nor does he provide a listing of these principles in *Guide of the Perplexed.* This lack has led some scholars to think that Maimonides backed away from stressing the importance of establishing a fixed set of dogmas. Other scholars have suggested that Maimonides wrote each of his works with different audiences in mind, so that it was not necessary for him to restate the Thirteen Principles in each of his later works.

The fact remains, though, that Maimonides's Thirteen Principles of Faith became a basic framework of understanding and teaching Judaism. Numerous poetic versions of the Thirteen Principles were composed, the most popular of which, the *Yigdal,* dates to the early fourteenth century. This hymn soon became part of the synagogue liturgy and appears in most Jewish prayer books to this day.

Let us turn now to a discussion of some of the major themes that relate to Maimonides's writings on faith and ethics.

The Nature of Faith

Maimonides begins his code of halakhah (Jewish law) by delineating the foundations of Jewish faith and ethics. Halakhah needs to be understood in the context of its underlying intellectual, spiritual, and moral principles.

The halakhah laws—and indeed the totality of Judaism—are premised on the existence of God, who gave the Torah to the Israelites. The first letters of the first four Hebrew words of Maimonides's code spell *Yod Heh Vav Heh*—the name of God intimately associated with the Israelites. Through this literary device, Maimonides signals that the foundation stone of religion in general, and of the halakhah in particular, is God.

Prior to composing the *Mishneh Torah,* Maimonides had compiled *The Book of Commandments,* which listed his enumeration of the 613 commandments of the Torah. The first commandment that Maimonides listed there, as rendered by Rabbi Moshe Ibn Tibbon, who translated this book from Arabic into Hebrew, is "to believe" in God. Yet, in the "Laws of Foundations of the Torah," Maimonides uses the phrase "to know" that God exists. The most likely explanation is that Maimonides did indeed stress the obligation "to know" God and that the translation "to believe" does not fully reflect Maimonides's thinking. What is the difference between belief and knowledge?

A person might believe in God with fullness of heart and mind; and yet, a belief—no matter how deeply held—is open to the implication that others might believe differently. Maimonides did not think that a person merely should believe in God, but rather that he should know God, should engage in philosophical proofs for the existence of God, should affirm—to the best of his intellectual capacity—the reality of God's being. To know God means to confront the ultimate Truth, a Truth that is universal and accessible to all wise people who engage in philosophical speculation.

For Maimonides, religion in its highest form demands rigorous intellectual activity. He eschews "blind faith" as a sign of ignorance. In his philosophical masterpiece, *Guide of the Perplexed*, he offers a poignant parable (3:51, pp. 618–620) about a ruler in his palace. The goal of the ruler's subjects is to gain access to him; various segments of the population achieve different results. Just as different subjects have different relationships with their ruler, so various segments of humanity have different relationships with God, the ultimate Ruler. The parable and its application are as follows.

There are some subjects who are outside the city, representing individuals without doctrinal belief and lacking rationality. They are far removed from the Ruler. Others are within the city but are facing away from the palace. They represent those who hold incorrect doctrinal beliefs. The further they walk, the further they move away from the palace. Those who seek to enter the palace but have not yet seen it are the "ignoramuses who observe the commandments." They appear to be pious, but since they are deeply deficient in their knowledge of God, Maimonides considers them "ignoramuses." Those who have reached the palace and circle around it to find a way in are people who study and observe halakhah but "who do not engage in speculation concerning the fundamental principles of religion and make no inquiry whatever regarding the rectification of belief." Another group consists of those who have entered the gate of the palace and walk in the antechambers; these people have engaged in proper philosophical analysis of the principles of religion and understand the natural sciences. Those who have entered the inner court and are in the presence of the Ruler have achieved demonstration in divine matters to the extent possible and are deeply steeped in philosophy and the natural sciences. Although these sages have reached the Ruler's inner court, they still might not hear the Ruler's voice. That gift is bestowed only on those who reach the highest level of metaphysical speculation and intellectual exertion. This last group of rare individuals represents the prophets, who actually hear God communicating with them.

Maimonides insists that piety must be linked to correct knowledge of God. In the opening section of his *Mishneh Torah*, he provides the philosophical basis of Jewish faith so readers will direct their efforts to entering the inner court of the Ruler. He does not want readers to be "ignoramuses who observe the commandments," but to be truly pious people who strive with all their ability to know God.

In the introduction to his commentary on the Mishnah, Maimonides emphasizes that human perfection requires both wisdom and proper action. A philosopher who acts immorally is defective, and so is one who follows the laws blindly without fathoming their spiritual underpinnings. "The purpose of the universe and all that is within it is—a wise and good person."

Bringing Religion in Line with Reason

As noted above, Maimonides believed that revelation, philosophy, and science could never be in genuine conflict because these bodies of knowledge derive from the same source: God. Thus, he devoted significant energy to harmonizing religion and reason whenever they appeared to be at odds with each other. Although he recognized the ultimate authority of the Jewish religious tradition, he posited that Judaism itself was founded on intellectually valid foundations.

Maimonides argued that philosophy was a basic ingredient in Judaism since antiquity, but that Jews had lost their philosophical traditions due to the various persecutions they had suffered over the centuries. He viewed his own work as reclaiming Judaism's original commitment to philosophy and reason. He sought to interpret the vast corpus of biblical and rabbinic literature in a rational and philosophically appropriate way and to explain the "irrational" passages so that they conformed to reason.

Marvin Fox, a scholar of Jewish thought and former chair of the Department of Near Eastern and Judaic Studies at Brandeis University, describes the unique greatness of Maimonides, the rabbi and philosopher: "We can learn first, and most importantly, from Maimonides an uncompromising and fearless intellectual honesty in all matters having to do with religion."[6] Maimonides, while fully devoted to the Jewish religious tradition, was also totally committed to intellectual exertion to gain a clear understanding of what that tradition actually teaches. Over the centuries, many erroneous ideas crept into Judaism due to ignorance and superstition; it was imperative to purge Judaism of these misguided beliefs and attitudes.

A powerful example of Maimonides's method of reconciling reason and revelation is found in his various discussions relating to the incorporeality of God. The Hebrew Bible and rabbinic literature are filled with language that refers to God as having physical and emotional attributes. Yet philosophy ruled out the notion of a corporeal God. God's essence and unity precluded God from having physical or emotional attributes, because these would limit God or make God subject to change. Maimonides thus needed to reinterpret all passages that referred to God in anthropomorphic or anthropopathic ways. He makes this point in the first section of *The Book of Knowledge* ("Foundations of the Torah" 1:11–12); moreover, he devotes much of the first book of *Guide of the Perplexed* to explaining biblical terms and passages that describe God as having physical or emotional characteristics. Maimonides's basic argument is that in the Hebrew Bible descriptions of God must be taken figuratively and metaphorically, not literally. The Hebrew Bible "speaks in the language of human beings." It wants readers to feel a strong attachment to its stories and ideas. If it had presented God in purely philosophical terms, the general public would not be able to relate to God in a meaningful way. The Hebrew Bible is intended for all people, not just for trained philosophers. Nevertheless, even the masses must be taught that God has no body and no emotions. They must hold philosophically true beliefs, even if they lack the intellectual sophistication to work out these truths on their own.

Maimonides was so insistent in denying God's corporeality that he considered those who held corporealist views to be apostates who have no place in the world to come ("Laws of Repentance" 3:7). The third of his Thirteen Principles of Faith is the negation of the corporeality of God. "All passages in Holy Scriptures that describe Him in physical terms, for example, walking, standing, sitting, speaking etc., these are all in metaphorical language."

Just as Maimonides insisted on the need to interpret biblical texts to conform to philosophy and reason, he similarly called for the interpretation of rabbinic statements that seemed to be irrational. In the Aggadah, the nonlegal portions of the Talmud, and in the Midrash, books of rabbinic homilies, the ancient sages often spoke of God in corporeal terms. They also presented parables and adages whose literal meanings might seem unfounded or absurd. In his introduction to *Perek Helek*, Maimonides writes of three groups, each with a different approach to the words of our sages.

The first group, which comprises the majority, consists of those who accept the words of our sages literally, without imagining any deeper meanings. These individuals believe their literalism is a sign of respect to the rabbis of antiquity. Yet, by taking everything literally, even when the words of the sages appear to violate reason, this group actually denigrates the sages. "The members of this group are poor in knowledge. One can only regret their folly. Their very effort to honor and to exalt the sages in accordance with their own meager understanding actually humiliates them." Maimonides concludes: "As God lives, this group destroys the glory of the Torah and extinguishes its light, for they make the Torah of God say the opposite of what it intended."[7]

A second group also takes the words of our sages literally; however, because many statements violate our sense of reason, this group concludes that the rabbis of antiquity were irrational and not worthy of intellectual credibility. This group dismisses the words of the sages. Maimonides rejects this viewpoint in strong terms.

A third group—so small that it hardly deserves to be called a group—consists of those who recognize the greatness of the sages and therefore seek the deeper meanings of their teachings. This group realizes that the sages hid profound wisdom in their statements and often spoke symbolically and in riddles. When a person discovers a rabbinic statement that seems to violate reason, the correct approach is to seek both its deeper meaning and its literary context. Was the statement a parable that needs interpretation? Was it hyperbole? Was it said in dramatic language in order to catch the attention of students and listeners? Was it said sarcastically, or in a humorous way? Without a careful literary analysis of rabbinic statements, it is quite probable that one will not really understand their meaning or intention.

Just as Maimonides argued that religion had to be brought into line with reason, he also recognized the limits of human reason. Philosophy (including science), though necessary for our intellectual life, does not have all the answers. An example of this is Maimonides's discussion of God's creation of the universe. He cites the Aristotelian view that posits the eternity of matter, hence precluding the possibility of God's creating the world from nothing. He rejects Aristotle's position because it cannot be proved to be true. Indeed, Maimonides believes that it is philosophically sound to argue that God created the universe from nothing. Given that we have no scientific or philosophical proof for the eternity of matter,

Maimonides thinks we must rely on biblical and rabbinic traditions that posit God as Creator. Revelation provides a truth that was not accessible through reason.

Interestingly, Maimonides notes that if philosophy and science could prove the eternity of matter, then he would interpret figuratively those biblical passages implying that God created the universe from nothing. "We should be very well able to give a figurative interpretation of those texts and to affirm as true the eternity of the world, just as we have given a figurative interpretation of those other texts and have denied that He, may He be exalted, is a body" (*Guide of the Perplexed* 2:25, p. 328).

It is clear, then, that Maimonides places a very high premium on human reason. While the divinely revealed text of the Hebrew Bible provides ultimate truth, this truth can only be deciphered through the mediation of reason. The ancient rabbinic sages are a vast repository of genuine wisdom, but this wisdom can only be accessed through a reasonable interpretation of their words. Maimonides believed that blind faith in the literal meaning of the sacred texts is not a sign of true faith, but a sign of folly. On the other hand, human reason is finite and hence unable to attain all Truth. At some point, it is revelation, and not reason, that guides the way. Maimonides notes that while human reason can comprehend a great deal, there are things that "it is not capable of apprehending in any way or through any cause; the gates of apprehension are shut before it.... Man's intellect indubitably has a limit at which it stops" (*Guide of the Perplexed* 1:31, p. 65).

For Maimonides, human perfection is achieved by apprehending God in as clear a manner as possible. In pursuing knowledge of God, we rely on the truths of revelation and the truths of reason. In Maimonides's view, the ideal person is not the philosopher but the prophet. A prophet must first attain the maximum truths available to a philosopher; then, God may or may not grant prophecy as a higher level of knowledge of God. Prophecy raises an already brilliant philosopher to a greater proximity with God. Different prophets reached different degrees of prophecy, with Moses having been granted the most intimate knowledge of God possible to any human being.

Maimonides discusses prophecy in general, and the supreme prophecy of Moses in particular, in chapters 7 and 8 of "Foundations of the Torah." He offers a vivid description of the nature of prophecy in the introduction to *Guide of the Perplexed*, where he uses the image of lightning to describe how people of differing intellects attain Truth. Humanity is in the midst of a dark night. When lightning flashes, people get a sudden glimpse of the reality that surrounds them. Moses, the premier prophet of all time, was on such a high spiritual level that it was as though the lightning flashed constantly for him. He could perceive reality as though the night had turned to day. Lesser prophets received fewer, less intense lightning flashes, thus perceiving far less than Moses, but far more than others who were not blessed with these flashes of insight.

Maimonides had the intellectual courage to push human reason to its limits, and the intellectual humility to know that human reason indeed has its limits.

God and Nature

For Maimonides, the phenomena of nature are reflections of the greatness of God, who created the laws of nature with infinite wisdom. Love and fear of God are derived from the contemplation of "His great and wondrous works and creatures" ("Foundations of the Torah" 2:2). As a rule, the laws of nature are fixed; the world follows its normal patterns.

What, then, is the nature of divine providence? Does God oversee the universe in an active way? Does God intercede with the natural flow of things?

Maimonides taught that God generally lets nature take its course. Active divine providence does not extend to inanimate objects or to animal life that lacks intellect, but rather is directly correlated to the development of a person's human intellect. Because God is the supremely perfect Intellect, God's providence overflows only to those whose intellects strive toward the Divine. Providence is the union of the divine Intellect with the human intellect. "Accordingly, everyone with whom something of this overflow is united will be reached by providence to the extent to which he is reached by the intellect" (*Guide of the Perplexed* 3:17, p. 474). Thus, providence is on a graduated scale. On the highest level, it relates to humans with the most developed intellects. It then diminishes in relation to those human beings with lesser intellects, diminishes further in relation to animal and plant life, and then reaches the lowest gradation in relation to inanimate objects. A human being whose intellect apprehends God on a high level will also experience God's providence on a high level. One whose intellect does not focus on God is thereby separated from God and "he becomes in consequence of this a target for every evil that may happen to befall him. For the thing that necessarily brings about providence and deliverance from the sea of chance consists in that intellectual overflow" (*Guide of the Perplexed* 3:51, p. 625).

Maimonides does not subscribe to the view that "this particular leaf has fallen because of a providence watching over it; nor that this spider has devoured this fly because God has now decreed and willed something concerning individuals" (*Guide of the Perplexed* 3:17, p. 471). In chapter 8 of his *Shemonah Perakim*, Maimonides refers to Talmudic passages that suggest God's imminent providence relating to all human actions, but he then cites the rabbinic dictum that the world operates according to its natural ways. He explains that when the rabbis said that humans rise and sit down in accordance with the will of God, "their meaning was that, when man was first created, his nature was so determined that rising up and sitting down were to be optional to him; but they did not mean that God wills at any special moment that man should or should not get up."[8]

Maimonides's view of divine providence might be understood by means of an analogy. The air is filled with radio waves, but we can only pick up these waves if we have a functioning radio with a proper antenna. If our radio or antenna is defective, it may receive no sounds or only sounds muffled by static. If we have a stronger radio and antenna, one can receive clearer sounds. If we have yet a stronger radio and antenna, we can receive clear sounds that have originated from distant places. In all of these cases, the radio waves have not changed at all. They have been constant. The level of reception has depended entirely on the power of the receiver to take in the radio waves. Similarly, God's divine intellect overflows all creation and is constantly present, but our ability to receive God's providence is correlated to the ability to tune in by means of the human intellect. The greater the intellectual apprehension of God, the greater the level of divine providence one experiences.

Maimonides understands prophecy in a similar vein. A prophet attains prophecy by developing his intellect and reaching a very high level of apprehension of God. At some point, the human intellect interacts with the divine intellect. While God ultimately grants the gift of prophecy—and may choose not to grant it—the gift comes only as a result of the prophet's own intellectual and spiritual exertions. "God turns whom He wills, whenever He wills it, into a prophet—but only someone perfect and superior to the utmost degree.... It is our fundamental principle that there must be training and perfection, whereupon the possibility arises to which the power of the Deity becomes attached" (*Guide of the Perplexed* 2:32, p. 362).

The blessings of the world to come are also viewed by Maimonides as being correlated to a person's intellectual and spiritual development. The greater a person's level of apprehension of God in this world, the greater will be that individual's bliss in the world to come. Those who hold false beliefs about God or who are among the wicked of this world will be cut off from life in the world to come and will simply cease to exist upon their deaths. Maimonides does not view the world to come in terms of rewards and punishments, but in terms of consequences. The consequence of righteousness and intellectual love of God is bliss in the world to come; the consequence of wickedness and false notions of God is not meriting the bliss in the world to come.

Direct Experience of God, Not Miracles, Is the Basis of Faith

The Hebrew Bible describes numerous miracles that God performs in which the laws of nature seem to have been overturned. Yet, philosophy and science see the laws of nature as being fixed and immutable. Thus, miracles—that is, supernatural violations of nature—should be impossible.

Maimonides believes that the laws of nature are manifestations of the will of God. Yet God has the power to intervene with these laws and to perform miracles—although God does so very rarely. To the extent possible, Maimonides interprets biblical and rabbinic descriptions of miracles as events that have natural explanations or that were presented in figurative, hyperbolic language. He scorns the ignorant folk who "like nothing better and, in their silliness, enjoy nothing more than to set the Torah and reason at opposite ends, and to move everything far from the explicable." These misguided people classify things as miracles, even when there are reasonable, scientific explanations available. "But I try to reconcile the Torah and reason, and wherever possible consider all things as of the natural order. Only when something is explicitly identified as a miracle, and reinterpretation of it cannot be accommodated, only then I feel forced to grant that it is a miracle."9

For Maimonides, biblical miracles could often be explained as highly unusual natural phenomena, rather than as supernatural events that defied the laws of nature. For example, locust plagues happen in the normal workings of nature; the plague of locusts in Egypt, though, was a particularly bad plague, above and beyond what usually occurred. Likewise, various "miracles" can be understood as natural phenomena that happened to take place at just the right time and place or that endured longer than usual.

Maimonides notes that the Talmudic sages themselves believed that miracles were, in a certain respect, part of nature rather than deviations from the natural laws. "They say that when God created that which exists and stamped upon it the existing natures, He put into these natures that all the miracles that occurred would be produced in them at the time when they occurred" (*Guide of the Perplexed* 2:29, p. 345). In other words, God implanted these "miracles" into the very fabric of the laws of nature at the time of creation. They were unusual phenomena that were created on a "time-release" basis—intrinsic features of nature, rather than violations of its laws.

Maimonides objected to the notion that the faith of Israel was based on miracles. On the contrary, the people of Israel did not follow Moses because of any miracles he performed. Faith based on miracles is flimsy; witnesses may eventually conclude that these "miracles" were the result of magic or illusion. The Hebrew Bible itself records various miracles such as the Ten Plagues in Egypt and the crossing of the Red Sea after which the witnesses of the miracles continued their evil and sinful ways. The miracles obviously did not convince them permanently of any divine truths.

Rather, Israel's faith is based on direct experience with God. When did the Israelites gain their trust in Moses's prophecies? "At the revelation at Mount Sinai, where our own eyes saw and our own ears heard the fire and the thunders and the flames. Moses went into the cloud and the voice [of God] spoke to him, and we heard" ("Foundations of the Torah" 8:1). The ancient Israelites had firsthand experience with God, and they passed down their story to the subsequent generations. We have the eyewitness testimony of hundreds of thousands of Israelites that God spoke to the people and gave them the commandments at Sinai. This—not miracles—is the basis for Jewish faith.

Maimonides's God: Bridging the Views of Philosopher and Rabbi

The God of the philosophers is infinitely remote—an impersonal Prime Mover or First Cause. The God of the Hebrew Bible and rabbinic tradition is infinitely near—a personal God who intervenes in human affairs. How did Maimonides the philosopher and Maimonides the rabbi bridge these two views of God?

As a philosopher, Maimonides knew that God is "without matter and is simple to the utmost degree of simplicity, whose existence is necessary, who has no cause and to whom no notion attaches that is superadded to His essence, which is perfect" (*Guide of the Perplexed* 1:58, p. 137). God is so utterly different and beyond anything humans can fathom, He is not describable by human words. Anything we say about Him is inadequate and incomplete. We can only say with some certainty what God is not: He is not a multiplicity, He is not material, He is not divisible, He is not bound to time or space. We must come to realize that God "cannot be apprehended by the intellects, and that none but He Himself can apprehend what He is" (1:59, p. 139). Maimonides is highly critical of poets and preachers who describe God with physical attributes, as though they actually have a clear idea of God—which Maimonides is sure they do not! "The utterances of some of them constitute an absolute denial of faith, while other utterances contain such rubbish and such perverse imaginings as to make men laugh when they hear them ... and to make them weep when they consider that these utterances are applied to God, may He be magnified and glorified" (1:59, p. 141).

Yet, Maimonides the rabbi knows full well that the Hebrew Bible contains prayers uttered to God by revered biblical personages and prophets; that rabbinic tradition sanctions—and requires—the daily recitation of prayers that include adulations of God referring to God as compassionate, gracious, and other similar terms. In Jewish tradition, God is "personal," accessible, capable of intervening in human events. Indeed, Maimonides surely recited the required prayers three times each day and presumably felt an emotional as well as an intellectual attachment to God. In his "Laws of Prayer" (4:15–16), he stresses the need for proper intention and concentration when praying. "One should clear his heart from all [extraneous] thoughts and see himself as though he stands before the Divine Presence. Therefore, one should sit down a bit before prayers, in order to focus the heart, and then pray with calmness and supplications."

Maimonides was able to maintain simultaneously both the philosophical and the biblical and rabbinic views of God. As Marvin Fox has correctly noted: "Maimonides is saying that our human condition leaves us no option but to live in the precarious situation in which we affirm and pursue in practice both a philosophically sophisticated conception of divine worship and a popular conventional pattern of prayer."[10] Maimonides demands the maintaining of a delicate balance that necessitates a dialectical tension; the philosopher must pray to religion's God, and the religionist must understand the God of the philosophers. Maimonides does not spell out how we are to accomplish this balancing act—only that we are required to do so.

The Torah and Commandments

Yeshaiahu Leibowitz, a twentieth-century Israeli philosopher, has wisely observed: "The very fact that the greatest philosopher of Judaism is the man who was its greatest halakhic [legal] authority is of an extremely profound significance."[11] He notes that there are scholars who see Maimonides primarily as a philosopher and others who view Maimonides primarily as a halakhist. In reality, he was both; he cannot be understood properly without taking both aspects into careful consideration.

As a philosopher, Maimonides sought to harmonize faith and reason to the extent possible. He applied his methodology to the interpretation of the Hebrew Bible and to the rationalizing of basic religious concepts such as providence, prophecy, the world to come, and miracles. Yet, as one of the greatest halakhic minds in Jewish history, Maimonides was deeply steeped in rabbinic lore and tradition. He was not only a brilliant philosopher; he was at the very same time a pious Jew dedicated to every detail of Jewish law. As we have seen in the previous discussion of Maimonides's views on prayer, he fostered a religious way of life that was intellectually sound and emotionally meaningful. Leibowitz has suggested that "the difference between Maimonides and the mere philosopher is that Maimonides's aim was a knowledge of God."[12]

Toward the end of *Guide of the Perplexed* (3:52, p. 630), Maimonides makes clear the essence of his philosophical and religious enterprise. The goal is to attain as full a relationship with God as possible, by both loving and fearing Him; this relationship is attained by means of the Torah. Maimonides viewed the Torah as teaching proper ideas about God that in turn lead to love of God, while the Torah's prescription of positive and negative commandments leads to fear of God. A person who attains a high level of apprehension of God is marked by proper intellectual and moral characteristics: "The way of life of such an individual, after he has achieved this apprehension, will always have in view loving-kindness, righteousness, and judgment, through assimilation to His actions, may He be exalted" (3:54, p. 638).

The Torah's commandments are essential ingredients in deepening our relationship with God. Maimonides insists that all the laws of the Torah were given by God with a purpose in mind: to provide for either the welfare of our souls or the welfare of our bodies. In caring for our souls, it provides correct opinions. In caring for our bodies, it ensures the proper functioning of society. "The letter of the Torah speaks of both perfections and informs us that the end of this Law in its entirety is the achievement of these two perfections" (3:27, p. 511). Even the biblical stories should not be viewed as superfluous folktales, but as essential sources of divine wisdom. Maimonides referred to biblical narratives as "mysteries of the Torah" and asserted: "Know that all the stories that you will find mentioned in the Torah occur there for a necessary utility for the Law; either they give a correct notion of an opinion that is a pillar of the Law, or they rectify some action so that mutual wrongdoing and aggression should not occur between men" (3:50, p. 613).

The People Israel and All Humanity: Repositories of Wisdom and Knowledge

Maimonides believed that the people of Israel, as receivers of the divine Revelation at Mount Sinai, have a key role in bringing God's word to all humanity. Interestingly, Maimonides avoids elaborating on Israel as "the chosen people" and does not include Israel's chosenness as one of the Thirteen Principles of Faith. Essentially, there is no difference between Jews and non-Jews; all have access to God, all have the opportunity to engage in philosophical speculation about the Deity, and all have the obligation to live righteously. Although there are post-Talmudic rabbinic texts that posit an ontological spiritual difference between Jews and non-Jews, Maimonides rejects this view outright. Menachem Kellner, professor of Jewish thought at the University of Haifa, has pointed out that Maimonides was radically opposed to any essentialist distinctions between Jews and other human beings.[13]

Maimonides makes his case clearly in "Laws of Sabbatical and Jubilee Years" (13:13). After describing the spiritual role given to the tribe of Levi, Maimonides writes that every human being, regardless of tribe or nationality, can serve God wisely and purely. As for anyone who does so, "Behold, this person has been totally consecrated, and God will be his portion and inheritance forever." All righteous people, whether Jewish or non-Jewish, have a place in the world to come.

Not only do non-Jews have access to God and to the world to come, but they also are repositories of wisdom and knowledge for the benefit of humanity—including Jews. In the introduction to his commentary on *Pirkei Avot*, Maimonides indicates that he has drawn from the wisdom of our rabbinic sages "as well as from the words of the philosophers, ancient and recent, and also from the works of various authors, as one should accept the truth from whatever source it proceeds."[14] Truth is not restricted to one ethnic or religious group but is the universal heritage of humanity. We all can learn from others.

Maimonides's argument goes further. Not only is wisdom the province of all human beings, but the Torah itself cannot be fully understood without knowledge of the universal wisdom of physics and metaphysics. To be a true scholar of Torah, a person must derive knowledge from all sources of universal wisdom, whether Jewish or non-Jewish. Marvin Fox has praised Maimonides's grand intellectual outlook as a needed antidote to the obscurantism and narrowness that sometimes characterizes religionists. Maimonides stands out as a beacon of light, "showing us that Judaism has nothing to fear from the best and most advanced sources of knowledge in any given age."[15]

Although Maimonides appreciated wisdom derived from non-Jews, he also believed that non-Jews needed to recognize that God—who gave the Torah to Israel—is the ultimate source of Truth. Maimonides expected non-Jews to accept the Seven Noahide Laws—basic laws of righteousness that the Hebrew Bible prescribes for humanity as a whole. Non-Jews who observe them purely on the basis on their own reason, and not because they were commanded by God, can be considered wise—but not righteous. Righteousness is specifically dependent on following the laws because they emanate from God and Torah.[16]

Although Maimonides rejects any inherent differences between Jews and non-Jews, he surely believes that Jews were granted a great boon by God when God gave the Torah to the people Israel. Maimonides viewed Jews as blessed through the Torah's teachings and commandments with a comprehensive path to God that helps them achieve philosophical truth and ethical behavior. He believed that centuries of adherence to the Torah have enabled Jews to develop a high level of spiritual wisdom, piety, and righteousness. As such, it is a responsibility of the Jewish people, bearers of God's Torah, to set an example of religious life at its best so the nations of the world may come to recognize the wisdom, truth, and righteousness of the One God.

Non-Jews, of course, may convert to Judaism and join the Jewish spiritual adventure as fellow Jews. While they do not need to convert to attain access to God, the door is open to those who sincerely wish to become proselytes. In an eloquent letter to Obadiah the proselyte, Maimonides assures the convert that he is to be counted among the disciples of Abraham. "There is no difference whatever between you and us ... for the Creator, may He be extolled, has indeed chosen you and separated you from the nations and given you the Torah. For the Torah has been given to us and to the proselytes."[17]

Religion and Superstition

Maimonides believed that true religion seeks to bring us closer to God through correct thought and proper deed. It is highly demanding of our intellectual, mental, and physical energy. Its goal is not to give us power over God, but to teach us to live in God's light and according to God's will. Conversely, superstition, which is antithetical to true religion, seeks to circumvent God's power by use of magical formulas or rituals. It does not demand philosophical or moral excellence; rather, it provides purported means to bypass or manipulate God to ward off evil or to attain a desired goal.

The Hebrew Bible prohibits turning to shamans or wonder-workers for guidance or help: "There shall not be found among you anyone ... who uses divination, a soothsayer, or an enchanter, or a sorcerer, or a charmer, or one who consults a ghost or a familiar spirit, or a necromancer. For whoever does these things is an abomination unto the Lord" (Deuteronomy 18:10–12).

For Maimonides, the source of superstitious belief is ignorance of the true nature of God. Superstitious people ascribe supernatural powers to venerated objects such as idols or believe in multiple divine powers. They rely on the magic and miracles of holy men and women or on magical rituals or objects. Because of their ignorance or fear, the superstitious do not turn directly to God but to idols and shamans.

Maimonides rules that it is forbidden to whisper a charm or read a biblical verse over a wound as a means of healing it. Nor may a person place a sacred object, such as a Torah scroll or tefillin (ritual objects worn by men during morning prayers) in a baby's crib so the child might sleep better. Such practices fall under the category of sorcery. Those who use the words and artifacts of religion in a superstitious way "are included among those who repudiate the Torah" ("Laws of Idolatry" 11:12).

Similarly, in "Laws of Mezuzah" (5:4), Maimonides chastises those who write the names of angels or saintly men, or other verses and charms, on the scrolls of their mezuzot. (A mezuzah is an encased parchment on which a scribe has written prescribed biblical passages; it is traditionally affixed to the doorposts of Jewish homes.) Such people "are included among those who have no share in the world to come. Those fools not only fail to fulfill the commandment, but they treat an important precept, which conveys God's Oneness as well as the love and worship of God, as if it were an amulet to benefit themselves." Although these people may think themselves to be pious, they are in fact egregious sinners who have forfeited their place in the world to come. Maimonides leaves no room for superstitious beliefs or behavior. He is emphatic in his opposition to talismans and amulets, just as he is unflinching in his repudiation of wonder-workers and shamans.

Maimonides was well aware that various rabbis and scholars had written approvingly of supernatural powers attributed to objects, meaning angels, demons, stars, and artifacts. In his *Epistle to Yemen*, he warns: "Do not consider a statement true because you find it in a book, for the prevaricator is as little restrained with his pen as with his tongue."[18] In his *Letter on Astrology*, he notes that "fools have composed thousands of books of nothingness and emptiness."[19] Later in the same letter, he warns: "It is not proper to abandon matters of reason that have already been verified by proofs.... A man should never cast his reason behind him, for the eyes are set in front, not in back."[20] It is possible that even sages were mistaken in their views; or that they spoke in allegorical language, not to be taken literally; or that they spoke within the context of their own time and place. Truth is to be based on reason and proof, not on the authority of sages who may or may not have correctly understood the matter at hand.

Maimonides insists that reason is the best bulwark against falling into an obscurantist mindset. It is religiously incorrect—and fatal to true religion—to promote superstitious beliefs and practices. Maimonides rejects a worldview that promotes uncritical thinking, blind surrender of intellectual autonomy to unworthy authorities, and reliance on "holy" wonder-workers. True religion demands intellectual integrity, personal responsibility, and the quest to relate to God directly, not through magical intermediaries.[21]

Moral Leadership

We have seen that Maimonides stands for an intellectually vibrant, philosophically compelling religious worldview. In his writings and teachings, he demonstrates an unflinching respect for reason—and a strong aversion toward those who do not use the gift of reason correctly. Although he often appears to be a stern and demanding philosopher, he also was a compassionate and caring rabbi.

In 1165, he wrote an *Epistle on Martyrdom* to the oppressed Jewish communities of Morocco. Fanatical Muslim rulers had coerced the Jews to either make a public affirmation of Islam or suffer death. Some chose martyrdom. Others outwardly professed Islam while living as crypto-Jews who maintained Judaism in secret. Maimonides encouraged the Jews to observe as many commandments as possible, assuring them that God would reward them for their faithfulness. Even if they were compelled to sin, they should not feel that they will be rejected by God, nor should they be made to feel guilty by fellow Jews. Their transgressions were committed under duress. While it would be best for them to leave for other lands where they could practice Judaism openly, they needed to do their best to maintain their Jewishness until such time as they could emigrate. Maimonides calls for a compassionate and sympathetic attitude toward those who had violated halakhah, including those who violated the Sabbath. "It is not right to alienate, scorn, and hate people who desecrate the Sabbath. It is our duty to befriend them, and encourage them to fulfill the commandments. The rabbis regulate explicitly that when an evil-doer who sinned by choice comes to the synagogue, he is to be welcomed and not insulted."[22]

In "Laws of Rebels" (3:3), Maimonides writes that those Jews who have rejected the faith and observances of the Torah would suffer the consequences in the eyes of God. But the children and grandchildren of these rebels were to be treated with compassion. Specifically referring to the descendants of Karaites—a sect that rejected the Oral Torah and rabbinic tradition—Maimonides indicates that "since they were born and raised among them [Karaites] according to their beliefs, such children are as captive babies among them.... Therefore it is fitting to bring them back in repentance and to draw them closer with words of peace until they return to the bastion of the Torah."

About the Translation

This volume includes my English translation of *The Book of Knowledge*, based on the Hebrew text prepared by Rabbi Mordecai Dov Rabinowitz (with commentary by Rabbi Shmuel Tanhum Rubinstein), published by Mossad HaRav Kook, Jerusalem, 1972, as volume 2 in the Rambam La-Am series. My translation of the Thirteen Principles of Faith is based on the Hebrew text prepared by Rabbi M. D. Rabinowitz, published as part of volume 18 of that series in 1961.

This volume includes the essential teachings of Maimonides as they appear in *The Book of Knowledge* and the Thirteen Principles of Faith. I have selected the passages that present those teachings that continue to be meaningful and relevant to modern readers. I have omitted passages that relate to outdated medieval scientific notions. I have also omitted passages that may seem redundant to modern readers. For example, although Maimonides offers multiple biblical verses in support of various teachings; I have generally only cited one proof text rather than all of them.

Since Hebrew does not always translate easily into English, I have sometimes paraphrased the Hebrew text so that it would read better in English. I have also added in brackets words that are not part of the Hebrew text but are needed to make the English text more comprehensible.

Maimonides was a medieval author who wrote for a male readership. He assumed that only a limited number of women would have the education or interest to read his work. This English translation, though, is obviously intended for a readership of women and men. Although I have attempted to make the English translation gender-neutral where possible, I have referred to God in the masculine form as Maimonides did. I have also used male pronouns to refer generically to humanity when I believed using "his or her" or similar such phrases would seem awkward. I ask readers— female and male—to understand that the text is directed to all of them.

Works Cited in the Commentary

In the course of the commentary, I have quoted various works of Maimonides that have been translated into English by others. All citations from the *Guide of the Perplexed* are from the translation of Shlomo Pines. Translations from the *Epistle on Martyrdom* and *Epistle to Yemen* are from Abraham Halkin and David Hartman, *Crisis and Leadership: Epistles of Maimonides*. Translations from the *Letter on Astrology* and other assorted writings are from Isadore Twersky, *A Maimonides Reader*. The quotation from Maimonides's letter to his student Joseph is from Raymond L. Weiss with Charles Butterworth, *Ethical Writings of Maimonides*.

I have quoted various scholars throughout the commentary, and in each case I indicate their names and the titles of the books cited. Full bibliographical information can be found at the end of this volume.

Advice to Readers

Please read (and reread) the text of the translation and commentary slowly and carefully. Maimonides is a serious sage who has much of value to teach us, and we benefit most if we ponder his words and mull over them. Studying Maimonides's essential teachings on Jewish faith and ethics is a spiritual and intellectual adventure—an adventure that can deepen and transform our lives.

Maimonides–
Essential Teachings on
Jewish Faith and Ethics

1 Maimonides begins his code of halakhah (Jewish law) by delineating the foundations of Jewish faith and ethics. Halakhah needs to be understood in the context of its underlying intellectual, spiritual, and moral principles.

2 Maimonides's description of God as the "First Being who brings into being all that exists" sounds very much like the God of the philosophers, that is, a Prime Mover who is not necessarily concerned with the ongoing operations of the world. A First Being or a Prime Mover implies a remote cosmic force, rather than a "personal" God to whom one might pray. By adding the phrase "blessed be He," Maimonides is indicating that the First Being is not an abstract and remote force, but is involved in our world. God is not only transcendent, but imminent. He is not only an incomprehensibly great and powerful force, but is related enough to us to inspire our blessings, our feeling of connectedness to Him.

In "Laws of Prayers" 4:15–16, Maimonides makes clear that prayer to God is of great importance to spiritual life. One must pray with proper concentration and devotion. "One should clear his heart from all [extraneous] thoughts and see himself as though he stands before the Divine Presence."

It seems that Maimonides is describing God in two seemingly contradictory ways. On the one hand, God is the First Being, the God of the philosophers. On the other hand, God is to be praised and worshipped as a "personal" God. Maimonides affirmed that both these conceptions are true, and that humans must relate to the Infinite and Eternal God in all His otherness—and in all His mysterious proximity. As Professor Marvin Fox has correctly noted, Maimonides teaches that our human condition compels us "to live in a precarious situation in which we affirm and pursue in practice both a philosophically sophisticated conception of divine worship and a popular conventional pattern of prayer" (Marvin Fox, *Interpreting Maimonides*, p. 319).

☐ Laws of Foundations of the Torah

Chapter One

1.   The foundation of foundations and the pillar of all wisdoms is to know[1] that there is a First Being who brings into being all that exists. All existing things from heaven to earth, and everything in between, only exist by virtue of the truth of His existence.

2.   If one were to posit that He does not exist, then nothing else could have come into being.

3.   If one were to posit that nothing else exists, He alone still exists and cannot be eliminated by their elimination because all things are contingent on Him; while He, blessed be He,[2] is not contingent on any of them. Thus, His trueness is not like the trueness of any one of them.

4.   This is what the prophet says: "And the Lord God Is truth" (Jeremiah 10:10). He alone is truth and nothing else is true in the same sense as He is true. This is what the Torah says: "There is nothing else aside from Him" (Deuteronomy 4:35); namely, there is no other existing truth aside from Him and like Him.

3   The astronomy of Maimonides's day posited the existence of heavenly spheres that existed above our physical world. These heavenly spheres were believed to be spiritual beings endowed with life. Ptolemaic astronomy charted the rotations of the stars and planets, which were believed to be governed by a primary, overarching sphere. Maimonides, basing himself on the best science available in his time, relied on the Ptolemaic system.

4   In describing the Revelation at Mount Sinai, the Torah records God's first words to the Israelites as "I am the Lord your God." Is this a statement or a commandment? While it seems merely to be an introductory statement, Maimonides interpreted it as a commandment—indeed, as the first of the Ten Commandments. We are commanded to know that "I am the Lord your God," to engage in intellectual pursuit of knowledge of God. Other rabbinic scholars, chief among them Rabbi Moses ben Nahman (1194–1270) of Barcelona, understood this verse as a statement. Knowledge of God is presupposed in the Torah, without the need for a specific commandment to know God.

For Maimonides, knowledge of God is not confined to philosophical inquiry. It also entails an experiential awareness of God's presence. In the *Guide of the Perplexed* (3:52, p. 629), Maimonides informs us that one seeking human perfection lives with the notion that "we are always before Him, may He be exalted, and walk about to and fro while His Indwelling is with us." This constant awareness of God's presence leads one to live humbly and piously.

5.   This Being is God of the universe, Master of the world. He governs the heavenly sphere[3] with an eternal and infinite power, a power that has no interruption. The sphere always rotates, and it is impossible for it to rotate without a Rotator. He, blessed be He, rotates it without a hand or body.

6.   Knowing this is a positive commandment, as it is stated, "I am the Lord your God" (Exodus 20:2).[4] Anyone who entertains the notion that there is another God transgresses a negative commandment, as it is stated, "You shall have no other gods before Me" (Exodus 20:3), and is a denier of the essential principle of faith; for this is the great principle upon which everything else depends.

<u>5</u> This verse—Deuteronomy 6:4—is the hallmark of Jewish faith: "Hear O Israel, the Lord is our God, the Lord is One." One of the first phrases taught to children when they first learn to speak, it is the last phrase uttered in one's confession before death. Jewish martyrs throughout the centuries have uttered this verse as their final proclamation of faith. The *Sh'ma,* as this verse is known, is included in the daily morning and evening prayers and is also recited before going to sleep and upon arising in the morning.

In his *Guide of the Perplexed* (1:58, p. 137), Maimonides notes that God is unlike His creations and "has nothing in common with them in any respect." Even his "oneness" is an absolute unity beyond our capacity to grasp fully. Since God is the ultimate Perfection, He is not describable by human words. Anything we say about Him is inadequate and incomplete. We can only say with some certainty what He is not: He is not a multiplicity; He is not physical; He is not divisible; He is not bound to space or time. We must recognize that God "cannot be apprehended by the intellects, and that none but He Himself can apprehend what He is" (*Guide of the Perplexed,* 1:59, p. 139).

Although we cannot philosophically reach a perfect understanding of the oneness of God, we are commanded to strive for as clear an understanding as we can achieve. On the experiential level, we can sense the presence of the One God.

7. This God is One, not two or more than two, but uniquely One unlike any other one existing in the universe: not like a one that contains many parts, and not one like a body that is divisible into sections and measurements, but rather a Unity unlike any other unity in the world. If the Creator had body and physicality, He would necessarily be finite because every physical body is finite. Our God, blessed be His Name, has infinite power that never ceases, so that [it is clear that] His power is not of a physical nature. Because He is not a body, He is not subject to physical characteristics, so He cannot be divided and separated; therefore, it is impossible that He be anything other than One. Knowledge of this matter is a positive commandment, as it is stated, "The Lord our God, the Lord is One" (Deuteronomy 6:4).[5]

8. It is explained in the Torah and Prophets that the Holy One, blessed be He, has no body or corporeal features, as it is stated, "For the Lord is God in the heavens above and on the earth below" (Deuteronomy 4:39); and a body cannot be in two places. It is stated, "To whom can you compare Me that I be similar" (Isaiah 40:25)? If He had a body, He would be similar to other physical beings.

6 According to Maimonides, it is an incontestable philosophical truth that God is incorporeal. Yet, the Bible includes many anthropomorphic references to God. Are philosophy and the Bible in conflict? Maimonides posits both the truth of philosophy and science and the truth of the Bible: both stem from the same Author, so there can never be an irreconcilable conflict between them. He resolves the problem of biblical anthropomorphisms by interpreting them as being expressions of a poetic, symbolic nature. In fact, God is absolutely incorporeal. The Bible uses anthropomorphic language not to deny God's incorporeality, but as a literary device. Maimonides cites a Talmudic passage (*Berakhot* 31b), reflecting the teachings of the school of Rabbi Yishmael, that the Torah speaks in the language of human beings; that is, it uses literary devices to make its message more intelligible to people. Anthropomorphisms, as figurative language, make the biblical text more vivid to readers and help them identify with God. If the Bible had used strictly philosophical and technical language, the masses would be unable to understand it and would be uninspired by its message. By speaking "in the language of humans," the Bible succeeds in being a living document with appeal to the broad spectrum of humanity.

7 Maimonides stresses the singular qualities of Moses as the ultimate prophet. Although even Moses could not grasp the fullness of God's truth, he was the human being who came closest. No one before or after him reached his level of intimacy with God.

Since the Torah was given by God through the agency of Moses, this would tend to support the view that Moses was a uniquely great prophet. Indeed, the Torah itself is popularly known as the Five Books of Moses.

Maimonides's insistence that Moses was the greatest prophet of all time, and that no one before or after him was on the same level, certainly had a polemical intent. It was to make clear to Jews, as well as to Christians and Muslims, that the Torah of Moses was the authoritative word of God, and no later prophet had the stature to abrogate it.

9. If so, what does it mean when the Torah states [in reference to God] "under His feet" (Exodus 24:10), "written by God's finger" (Exodus 31:18), "the hand of God" (Exodus 9:3), "the eyes of God" (Genesis 38:7), "the ears of God" (Numbers 11:1), and similar such phrases? This is all according to the understanding of human beings, who only comprehend physical things; and the Torah speaks in the language of human beings.[6] These are all metaphorical expressions. Human intelligence is unable to grasp and fathom His essence.

10. What did Moses seek when he asked "Please show me Your glory" (Exodus 33:18)? He sought to know the truth of the nature of the Holy One, blessed be He, until his heart fully comprehended Him. God replied that no living human being has the capacity to attain the full truth of God's essence. God informed him of things that no other human being before or after would receive, so that [Moses] attained unique knowledge of God's essence, albeit incomplete knowledge, as though only seeing "the back" of God.[7]

11. Since it has been explained that He is not corporeal or physical, it is clear that He is not subject to physical attributes: no attaching and no separating; no location and no measurement; no ascending and no descending; no right and no left; no front and no back; no sitting and no standing. He is not bound to time so that He would have had a beginning and an end limited by years. He does not change, and there is nothing that can cause Him to change. He is not subject to death or life in the same way as a living body. He has no gradations of wisdom akin to human wisdom. He is not subject to sleeping or awaking, anger or laughter, happiness or sadness, silence or words resembling the words of humans.

8 Maimonides, relying on the prevailing views of ancient Greek philosophers, thought that the universe was geocentric. He followed the system developed by the Hellenistic astronomer Claudius Ptolemaeus of the second century CE. The Ptolemaic system had Earth at the center, with spheres moving outward from Earth in the following order: moon, Mercury, Venus, the sun, Mars, Jupiter, Saturn, fixed stars, and finally the sphere of the Prime Mover. It was believed that while matter on Earth was subject to decay and death, the heavenly spheres were eternal. Maimonides, in line with prevailing religious views of the time, believed that the spheres became more spiritual as they ascended toward the sphere of the Prime Mover. He attributed "life" to the heavenly spheres, meaning that they had a consciousness of God. Angels—who were purely spiritual beings—were on a rung higher than the fixed stars. Maimonides provides a detailed discussion of cosmology and the earthly elements in chapters 3 and 4 of this section of the *Mishneh Torah*. I have omitted these sections in my translation because advances in scientific knowledge have eclipsed the ancient and medieval theories. This is very much in accord with Maimonides's own view that religion should be interrelated with the best available scientific knowledge of the times.

12. Because this is so, all these things and their likes [anthro-pomorphisms and anthropopathisms] that are mentioned in the Torah and Prophets are all metaphorical and rhetorical language. He, blessed be He, is above and beyond all these [physical attributes and descriptions].

Chapter Two

1. It is a commandment to love and fear this honored and awesome God, as it is stated, "And you shall love the Lord your God" (Deuteronomy 6:4) and "You shall fear the Lord your God" (Deuteronomy 6:13).

2. What is the way to love and fear Him? When a person contemplates His wondrous and great works and creations, and he sees in them His infinite wisdom, immediately he loves and praises and exalts and yearns with an overwhelming yearning to know His great Name, as David said, "My soul thirsts for God, the living God" (Psalm 42:3). On meditating these very things, one immediately recoils, fears, and trembles, realizing that he is a tiny, low, and obscure being of small intelligence standing before the One with perfect wisdom, as David said, "When I see Your heavens and the works of Your hands ... what is a human being that You should take notice" (Psalm 8:4–5)?

8. The angels and heavenly bodies live and recognize the Creator, knowing Him with an exceedingly great intelligence.[8] Even those on the first level are unable to apprehend the truth of the Creator in His essence; yet, they apprehend and know more than the lower levels of these spiritual forms. Those on the tenth and lowest level also apprehend the Creator in a manner that human beings, composed of earthly matter and form, cannot equal.

9 In the first chapter of the book of Ezekiel, the prophet relates his vision of the Divine Throne of Glory. He saw four mysterious creatures, each with four faces, right under the Divine Throne. Rabbinic tradition (Mishnah *Hagigah* 2:1) thought of this vision as representing a sort of chariot, with God's Throne being upheld by the four angelic creatures; the first chapter of Ezekiel was thus described as the Account of the Chariot (*Ma'aseh Merkavah*). This term came to designate the speculations, visions, and discussions relating to the esoteric wisdom relating to God and His Throne of Glory. Maimonides employs the term as referring to the philosophical speculations about the nature of God.

9.   All beings, from the holiest angel to the tiniest mosquito, exist
by virtue of His truth. Since He knows Himself and recognizes
His greatness, majesty, and truth, He knows everything. There
is nothing hidden from Him.

10.   The Holy One, blessed be He, recognizes and knows His truth as
it is. He does not know by means of an external knowledge that is
separate from Him, the way we know things, because we and our
knowledge are not identical. But as for the Creator, may He be
blessed, He—His knowledge and existence are absolutely One.
He is the Knower, the Known, and the Knowledge itself—One.
The mouth has not the power to verbalize this adequately, nor
the ear to comprehend this, nor the heart to understand it fully.

11.   That which we have discussed in these two chapters is like a
drop in the ocean compared to what is required to explain these
matters. The full explanation of the principles discussed in these
two chapters is called the "Account of the Divine Chariot."**9**

12.   Our ancient sages commanded that one may not teach these
matters [the Account of the Divine Chariot] except to one
person at a time, and only to he who is wise and capable of
independent analysis. Even then, one may only teach chapter
headings and a smattering of the matter, and the student will
then make the necessary inferences and attain its full depth of
meaning. These matters are extremely deep, and not every
mind is able to absorb them.

Chapter Four

10.   All our discussion [relating to angels and the heavenly
spheres] is like a drop in the bucket. They are deep matters,
although not as profound as [the Account of the Chariot].

(continued on page 15)

10 The Talmud (*Hagigah* 14a) relates that four sages entered the "Orchard" (*pardes*), a metaphor for the realm of mystical speculation. As a result of this overwhelming experience, Ben Azzai died, Ben Zoma lost his mind, and Elisha ben Abuya became a heretic. Only Rabbi Akiva entered and left the Orchard in peace. If the Orchard had proved to be so dangerous to great sages, then obviously it is perilous for ordinary people to speculate in metaphysical matters.

Although Maimonides provides this warning to his readers, he does so only at the end of chapter 4, after he has already introduced topics from the Orchard. Perhaps he assumes that his cursory discussion of these issues does not constitute actually entering the Orchard. He also assumes that his readers are already religiously observant people devoted to the fulfillment of the commandments relating to what is permitted and what is forbidden. They are, therefore, better prepared to deal with the metaphysical topics, even if only on a superficial level. Alternatively, perhaps Maimonides believes that all thinking people should be exposed to the topics of the Orchard, whether or not their stomachs "are filled with bread and meat." However, they should be warned not to get too deeply involved in metaphysical speculation until they are well rooted in the practices of the halakhah.

These are known as the "Account of Creation." Our sages commanded that one may not teach these matters in public but may only teach it and explain it to one person at a time.

11.   What is the difference between the Account of the Chariot and the Account of Creation? The Account of the Chariot is not taught even to one person unless that person is wise and capable of independent analysis; [even then] one only teaches chapter headings. The Account of Creation may be taught to an individual, even one who is not capable of independent analysis, and may be explained as fully as possible. Why are these things not taught in public? Because not every person has an expansive enough intelligence to grasp the explanations of these things fully.

12.   When a person contemplates these things and recognizes all the creations—angels, heavenly spheres, human beings, and so forth—and the wisdom of the Holy One, blessed be He, in each of the creations, his love for God will increase. His soul will thirst and long to love God, blessed be He. He will fear and tremble from his own smallness, inadequacy, and insignificance when he compares himself to the great holy creations [the heavenly bodies] and most certainly to one of the spiritual forms [angels] that have no physical qualities at all. He will find himself to be like a vessel filled with shame and humiliation, empty and deficient.

13.   The topics of the first four chapters dealing with these five commandments [to know that there is a God, that He is the only God, that He is a perfect unity, to love God, and to fear God] were called by our ancient sages "the Orchard," as it is said, "Four entered the Orchard" (*Hagigah* 14a).[10] Even though

(continued on page 17)

[11] Although under certain circumstances one should choose martyr-dom, Maimonides had sympathy for those who capitulated to the demands of their oppressors. He wrote letters to the Jews of Morocco and the Jews of Yemen, both communities having been confronted with the choice of forceful conversion to Islam or death. Maimonides urged Jews to leave these countries rather than to live under such duress. If they were unable to leave, they should maintain as much Jewish religious practice as possible and remain hopeful of their ulti-mate redemption. In the case of the Jews of Morocco, Maimonides was informed that the rulers forced Jews to make a verbal profession of faith in Islam but did not enforce behavior patterns. Thus, Jews could still manage to observe their Judaism in private. Although mar-tyrdom would be a noble choice even in this situation, Maimonides wrote: "But if anyone comes to ask me whether to surrender his life or to acknowledge [Islam], I tell him to confess and not choose death" (Abraham Halkin and David Hartman, *Crisis and Leadership,* p. 30).

One of the tragic elements in Jewish history has been the ongoing religious oppression that Jews have suffered in Christian and Muslim lands. When religious zealotry held sway, the Jews, a tiny and defense-less minority group, were easy targets for fanatical religious leaders and their masses of followers. Through the centuries, many thousands of Jews paid with their lives rather than be forcibly converted to another religion. Many other thousands of Jews were forcibly con-verted. While the vast majority of these converts eventually lost their Jewish identities entirely, a significant group maintained their Jewish-ness by living as crypto-Jews. During the course of history, including in our own days, thousands of descendants of crypto-Jews have returned to the faith of their ancestors.

[these four] were great sages of Israel and very wise, not all of them had the power to know and understand these things fully. I say it is not fitting to walk in the Orchard unless one has first filled his stomach with bread and meat, that is, to know what is forbidden and what is permitted, and so forth, of all the other commandments. It is proper to give them [the other commandments] precedence because they cultivate one's understanding first. Moreover, they are the great good which the Holy One, blessed be He, has intended for the habitation of this world so that one will inherit life in the world to come. These things may be known by all, whether adult or child, man or women, one of broad or one of narrow spirit.

Chapter Five

1. All members of the house of Israel are commanded to sanctify this great Name, as it is stated, "And I shall be sanctified among the children of Israel" (Leviticus 22:32); and are warned not to desecrate it, as it is stated, "And you shall not desecrate My holy Name" (Leviticus 22:32). How is this applied? If an idolater should come and force an Israelite to transgress any one of the Torah's commandments on pain of death, [the Israelite] should transgress and not be murdered, as it states about the commandments, "that a person may observe them and live by them" (Leviticus 18:5). "And live by them" [implies] that one should not die by them. One who chooses to die rather than transgress is liable for his own death.[11]

[12] The biblical book of Daniel tells the story of Daniel and his three friends, talented, young exiled Judean nobles who were put into royal service in the Babylonian court of King Nebuchadnezzar. Through his skill at interpreting Nebuchadnezzar's dream, Daniel was appointed to a high position, and his companions likewise were given high offices. Hananyah, Mishael, and Azaryah refused to bow down to a golden idol that the king had set up; as a punishment, Nebuchadnezzar had them thrown into a fiery furnace. Miraculously, they were unharmed, and the king restored them to their offices.

Daniel continued his royal service to Darius, Nebuchadnezzar's successor. Jealous rivals, knowing of Daniel's strong Jewish faith, had a law passed that required everyone to worship only the king for a period of thirty days. Daniel refused to comply with this law, continuing instead to pray to God three times each day according to Jewish practice. As punishment, he was cast into a lions' den; miraculously, he emerged unharmed by the lions. Darius then appointed Daniel back to his high post.

Daniel, Hananyah, Mishael, and Azaryah thus became classic heroes of Jewish faith. They were willing to risk their lives rather than worship foreign gods.

After the destruction of the Second Temple in Jerusalem by the Romans in 70 CE, the Jews were subjected to harsh oppression. Many were sent into exile, and many others were sold into slavery. Rabbi Yohanan ben Zakkai succeeded in establishing a rabbinic academy in Yavneh, maintaining continuity of Jewish religious life in the land of Israel. During the next generation, a rebellion against Rome developed, led by a charismatic Jewish warrior known as Bar Kokhba. Rabbi Akiva, the most influential sage of his generation, was deeply involved in the rebellion and viewed Bar Kokhba as a messianic figure. When a full-blown revolt erupted (132–135 CE), the Romans crushed the Jewish forces. The Roman emperor, Hadrian, enacted cruel policies against the remaining Jews, including a prohibition against teaching Torah in public. Rabbi Akiva defied this rule; he was imprisoned by the Romans and ultimately was tortured to death in Caesarea. His last words were

(continued on page 20)

2.   When does this apply? Only in regard to those commandments other than idolatry, sexual immorality, and murder. In regard to these three sins, if an Israelite were told to transgress or be murdered, he should choose to be murdered rather than transgress. When does this [distinction between these three commandments and the other commandments] apply? At a time when the idolater's intention is for his own benefit. For example, if he forced [the Israelite] to build him a house on the Sabbath, or to cook his food [on the Sabbath], or if he forced a Jewish woman to cohabit with him, and so forth. If his intention was solely to make [the Israelite] transgress the commandments, then if this was in private without the presence of ten Israelites, the person should transgress and not be murdered; but if [the Israelite] was forced to transgress in the presence of ten Israelites, then he should be murdered rather than transgress, even if [the idolater] intended to make [the Israelite] transgress any of the other commandments.

3.   The above discussion refers to a time when there is no general persecution of Jews. But at a time of persecution—if, say, an evil king like Nebuchadnezzar and his colleagues arise and make decrees to annul Judaism or one of its commandments—one should forfeit life rather than transgress even one of the other commandments, whether forced in the presence of ten Israelites or in private.

4.   Anyone who was supposed to transgress rather than be murdered, but chose to be murdered rather than transgress, is liable for his own death. Anyone who was supposed to be murdered rather than transgress, who indeed was put to death rather than transgressing, has sanctified God's Name.[12] If this was in the presence of ten Israelites, he has sanctified the Name

(continued on page 21)

the *Sh'ma,* proclaiming the unity of God (*Berakhot* 61b). According to Jewish tradition, Rabbi Akiva was one of ten rabbis put to death by the Romans in the uprising's aftermath. The Talmud lauds the martyrdom of Rabbi Akiva and his colleagues as reflecting the highest level of sanctification. (See *Bava Batra* 10b and *Sanhedrin* 110b.)

in public as did Daniel, Hananyah, Mishael, and Azaryah, and Rabbi Akiva and his colleagues. These are martyrs of the highest level. Anyone who was supposed to be murdered rather than transgress, but transgressed rather than be murdered, has desecrated the Name. If this was in the presence of ten Israelites, he has desecrated the Name in public. He has not fulfilled the positive commandment of sanctifying the Name and has transgressed the negative commandment forbidding desecrating the Name. Nevertheless, because he transgressed through coercion, he is not subject to [the punishment of] lashes and is certainly not subject to the death penalty by a human court, even if he had been coerced into murdering someone. [A human court] may not give lashes nor the death penalty except to one who has sinned willfully, in the presence of witnesses and after having received due warning [not to commit the sin]. If one commits the most heinous sin of idolatry due to coercion, he is not subject to the punishment of excision [whereby his soul is cut off by God], nor is he subject to capital punishment by a human court. So much more so is [one exempt from punishment] if coerced to violate any of the other commandments of the Torah.

[13] Maimonides bases this ruling on sources in the Babylonian Talmud, *Terumot* 8:12, and in the Jerusalem Talmud, *Terumot* 8:4. The under-lying principle is that no one has the right to sacrifice the life of another person, and no group may sacrifice one of its members to save them-selves. This ruling fosters strong solidarity among group members. Their standing together, rather than surrendering any one of them to the enemy, may discourage the enemy from acting against them at all. Or, it might stimulate the group to stand together in their joint defense against the enemy.

In the case of Sheva ben Bikhri, who was guilty of the death penalty for rebelling against King David (2 Samuel 20), it was permissible to turn over the villain to save the others.

These laws reflect the difficult conditions under which Jews lived and their need to develop strategies to stay united against the oppressions they suffered.

[14] One who was compelled by an oppressor to violate the three cardinal sins is not punishable by human courts. But one who voluntarily trans-gressed these sins as a means of curing an illness is punishable by human court.

5.	If idolaters said give us one of your women for us to defile or we will defile all your women, let all the women be defiled rather than turning over one Israelite. Likewise, if idolaters said "Give us one of you so that we may murder him or we will murder all of you," let them all be murdered rather than turning one Israelite over. If [the oppressors] specify [the Israelite they want to murder], saying, "Hand over so-and-so or we will murder all of you"—if the [specified person] was in fact guilty of the death penalty, as was Sheva ben Bikhri—then they may turn him over, but we do not initially instruct them to do so. If [the specified person] was not guilty of the death penalty, let them all be murdered rather than turning over one Israelite.[13]

6.	Just as [the sages] distinguished [between the three cardinal sins and all other sins] in matters of coercion, so they distinguished in matters of illness. How is this applied? If a person was ill and on the verge of death, and the doctors said that the cure depends on transgressing a Torah law, they may violate any of the commandments of the Torah to heal one who is in danger, with the exception of idolatry, sexual immorality, and murder. Even in a situation of grave danger, these [three commandments] may not be used as a cure. If one transgresses [one of these three sins] for a cure, the court punishes him accordingly.[14]

7.	How do we know that one may not violate any of these three commandments even when one's life is in danger? It is stated: "You shall love the Lord your God with all your heart and all your soul and all your might" (Deuteronomy 6:5), teaching that [you are to love God] even if your life is at stake. Also, human intelligence indicates that one should not murder one human being to save another human being. The [gravity of the sin of] sexual immorality is akin to that of murder.

15 Mixed plantings in vineyards are forbidden by the Torah (Deuteronomy 22:9); it is not only forbidden to plant grains in a vineyard, but it is also prohibited to derive benefit from such plantings. The prohibition of mixing meat and milk is derived from the threefold repetition of the verse forbidding seething a kid in the milk of its mother (Exodus 23:19, Exodus 34:26, and Deuteronomy 14:21). The prohibition extends to cooking, eating, or deriving benefit from meat and milk cooked together. Although one is normally not allowed to benefit from "mixed plantings of vineyards" or from meat and milk cooked together, the prohibitions are waived if these items are needed in the cure of life-threatening illnesses.

8.   When is it forbidden to transgress all the prohibitions [except for the three cardinal sins] to cure one who is dangerously ill? This refers to when these [transgressions] are experienced in a usual manner that gives pleasure, such as feeding a sick person unclean creatures and reptiles, or bread on Passover, or food on the Day of Atonement. However, if [forbidden items] are [used as cures] not in a usual manner that gives pleasure, such as using [forbidden foods] to make a plaster or salve, or having the sick person drink bitter-tasting medications made with forbidden foods, this is permissible even in nondangerous illness because the [ill person] derives no pleasure of taste. The exceptions to this are mixed plantings in vineyards and mixtures of meat and milk, both of which are forbidden even where no pleasure is derived [in consuming them]; these may only be used in cases of danger [to life].**15**

10   Anyone who willfully, disparagingly, and spitefully transgresses a Torah commandment without being coerced desecrates the Name. If one did so in the presence of ten Israelites, he has desecrated the Name in public. If one avoided transgressing or fulfilled a commandment not for ulterior motive—not because of fear or terror, not to gain honor, but only because of the command of the Creator, blessed be He, such as when Joseph the Righteous held himself back from his master's wife —one has sanctified the Name.

16 One who follows the letter of the law may be said to be a good and just person. However, a pious and righteous person will hold himself to a higher standard and will go beyond what the law demands. Optimally, all people should strive to include themselves in the categories of piety and righteousness.

17 Tefillin (phylacteries) are generally worn by men during morning prayers, although some very pious men may wear the tefillin throughout the day. Tefillin have two parts. The first is a small leather box holding a parchment with verses from the Torah that is fastened to one's upper arm. A long strap is then wound around the arm and hand. A second small leather box, which holds four parchments with verses from the Torah, is placed centered on the wearer's head, just above the hairline. The Torah alludes to tefillin in Deuteronomy 6:8 and 11:18, when it instructs: "And you shall bind them [the words of Torah] as a sign upon your arm, and they shall be as frontlets between your eyes."

11.   There are other things that are included in the category of
      desecration of the Name. If a person great in Torah knowledge
      and distinguished for piety does things that cause people to
      talk negatively about him—even if these things are not
      transgressions—he has desecrated the Name. Examples of this
      are: if one purchases an item and does not pay for it immediately
      when he has money with which to pay and the creditor is
      seeking payment, and yet he puts off the creditor; or when he
      overly indulges in laughing, eating, or drinking among ignorant
      people; or if he speaks rudely to others and does not receive them
      with a kind countenance, but rather with contentiousness and
      anger; and so forth. The greater the sage, the more scrupulous
      he should be, and he should go beyond what the law
      demands.[16] On the other hand, if the sage is scrupulous in his
      behavior, and he speaks pleasantly with others and receives
      them with a kind countenance; if he is affronted but does not
      affront others; if he honors others, even those who deal lightly
      with him; if he conducts his business with honesty; if he does
      not overly indulge in eating with the ignorant or being in their
      company; if he is always seen as being engaged in Torah,
      wrapped in the ritual fringes, and crowned with tefillin,[17]
      conducting himself beyond what the law demands without
      greatly distancing himself [from others] and not being
      insensitive to them, so that everyone praises him and loves him
      and strives to emulate his deeds—he has sanctified the Name.
      About him, the verse states, "And He said to me, you are my
      servant, Israel, and I am glorified through you" (Isaiah 49:3).

18 When holy texts are "put aside," they are placed in a storage area rather than being destroyed by hand. This is a sign of reverence for the texts. It is an ancient and widespread Jewish custom to take these texts, once their condition has deteriorated seriously, and bury them respectfully in the cemetery.

Chapter Six

1. One who erases any of the holy and pure Names by which the Holy One, blessed be He, is known is liable to receiving lashes according to Torah law. In speaking of idolatry, [the Torah] states, "And you shall erase their names [that is, the names of idolatrous gods] from that place; do not do such to the Lord your God" (Deuteronomy 12:3–4).

8. It is forbidden to burn or destroy by hand the Holy Scriptures, or their translations and commentaries. This refers to Holy Scriptures written in holiness by a Jew. But if a heretical Jew wrote a Torah scroll, it is burnt together with the Names of God on it because that [heretic] does not believe in the holiness of the Name and did not write His name [with holy intention], but rather he considers [the Torah] to be like any other book. Because he believes this way, the name of God was not sanctified [when he wrote God's names], and it is a positive commandment to burn [the scroll]. This is to prevent giving positive reputation to heretics or the works of their hands. If an idolater wrote the Name, it is put aside. Holy Scriptures that become worn out, or that were written by idolaters, are put aside.[18]

19 For Maimonides, the prophet had to be an intellectually gifted individual who attained a high level of understanding of God. Indeed, the prophet first had to be a philosopher before being granted the gift of prophecy by God. In his introduction to *Guide of the Perplexed*, Maimonides notes that the human mind cannot reach a full understanding of the divine mysteries. He draws on the image of lightning to describe how different intellects attain aspects of Truth. Humans are engulfed in darkness. When lightning flashes, they get a sudden glimpse of reality, but the illumination from the flashes does not last long. The greatest prophet, Moses, achieved such a lofty level that it was as though the lightning flashed constantly for him. Lesser prophets received fewer numbers and lesser degrees of flashes, thus perceiving less than Moses—but more than those who were not blessed at all with these flashes of insight.

Maimonides's view of prophecy was in line with his insistence on the intellectual and philosophical basis of one's relationship with God. For him, it would be inconceivable for God to communicate with a human being, unless that human being had reached a very high level of philosophical comprehension of the Almighty. Yet, there is nothing in the biblical text itself that compels one to adopt Maimonides's view. On the contrary, the Bible never describes prophets as being philosophers; indeed, some seem to have been simple shepherds. Prophets are distinguished for being visionaries deeply committed to righteousness and justice, not for their philosophical proclamations. Maimonides's discussion of prophets and prophecy is clearly shaped by his philosophical views, rather than having emerged from a plain reading of the biblical text.

Chapter Seven

1. It is a foundation of faith to know that God endows humans with prophecy. Prophecy only takes hold on a sage who is very great in wisdom and strong in character; one whose [evil] inclination never controls him, but rather who is always in control of his inclination; a person of expansive knowledge and logical thinking.**19** A person endowed with these qualities, [and also] physically complete, when he enters the Orchard [of spiritual contemplation of the divine mysteries]—[when he] clings to these profound and great matters, and has a clear mind to understand and perceive; and sanctifies himself; and separates himself from the masses of the people who walk in the darkness of the mundane; and prods himself and teaches his soul to avoid even one thought about idle matters and ephemeral nonsense and material concerns, but rather keeps his mind always directed heavenward, linked to the Divine Throne to contemplate the [heavenly] holy and pure forms; and perceives the wisdom and greatness of the Holy One, blessed be He, from the highest form [angels] to the lowliest of earthly forms—immediately the holy spirit rests on him. His soul then intermingles with the level of angels, and he becomes another person. He realizes he is no longer the same as he used to be but has been elevated to a higher spiritual level than other human beings.

2. The prophets are of various levels. Just as in wisdom, one sage has more than another, so in prophecy, one prophet may be greater than another prophet. All of them attain prophetic vision only in a dream in a revelation at night, or during the day after they have fallen into a trance, as it is stated, "I am known to him in a vision, in a dream I speak to him" (Numbers 12:6). When they prophesy, their limbs tremble, and the power of the body goes limp, and their perceptions become confused—but their intellects remain lucid so as to understand the vision.

[20] Maimonides's stress on the unique greatness of Moses may well have been influenced by the religious polemics of his day. Christianity claimed that Moses's Torah was eclipsed by Jesus; Islam claimed that Moses's Torah was eclipsed by Muhammad. Maimonides, therefore, underscored the belief that Moses was the supreme prophet. No one before or after could reach his level. No one before or after could alter or improve upon the prophecy he received from God.

3. The things conveyed to the prophet during prophecy are transmitted by means of parable; and the interpretation of the parable is immediately etched into his heart so that he will know what it means.

4. Prophets cannot prophesy whenever they wish. Rather, they must concentrate their minds and be in a spirit of happiness and good-heartedness, meditating while being alone. Prophecy does not imbue [the prophet if he is] in a spirit of sadness or idleness, but only in happiness.

6. All these things that we have stated about prophecy refer to all the earlier and later prophets—but not to Moses our teacher, the leader of all prophets.[20] What is the difference between the prophecy of Moses and that of all other prophets? All prophets prophesied in a dream or vision, but Moses prophesied while he was awake and standing upright. All the other prophets [received prophecy indirectly] through an angel and therefore perceived their visions in parables and riddles. But Moses received [prophecy directly] not through an angel and not through parable, but perceived his vision clearly without riddle or parable. All the prophets feared, trembled, and wilted; Moses did not, but communicated with God "as a person speaks to his friend" (Exodus 33:11). Just as a person is not afraid to hear the words of a friend, so Moses our teacher had the mental power to understand the words of prophecy while remaining fully in control of himself. The other prophets could not prophecy whenever they wished, but Moses was not like this; whenever he wished, the divine spirit would cover him and prophecy would befall him. He did not need to concentrate his mind and prepare for prophecy because he was always mindful and prepared, ready like an angel of God.

21 Miracles presented something of a philosophical dilemma for Maimonides. He believed that the laws of nature were put into place by a perfect and omniscient God. It was philosophically problematic to maintain that God would need to intervene and defy the laws of nature by means of miracles. Yet, the Bible contains many stories of miracles performed by God. In deference to the authority of the Bible, Maimonides conceded that God did indeed sometimes perform miracles that overrode the laws of nature. In deference to the authority of philosophy and science, he conceded that God performed supernatural miracles rarely, and only when the occasion absolutely required it. In his *Epistle on Resurrection*, Maimonides criticizes those who, in their ignorance, claim that things are miracles when they are actually natural occurrences. "But I try to reconcile the Torah and reason, and wherever possible consider all things as of the natural order. Only when something is explicitly identified as a miracle, and reinterpretation of it cannot be accommodated, only then I feel forced to grant that it is a miracle" (Halkin and Hartman, *Crisis and Leadership*, p. 223).

7. A prophecy might descend on a prophet solely for his own use. It might intend to expand his sensitivity and to increase his knowledge so that he might become aware of some great matter of which he had previously been unaware. It is also possible a prophet will be sent to the general public or to a city or kingdom to instruct people about what they should do, or to prevent them from continuing in their evil ways. When a prophet is sent on a mission, he is given a sign or wonder so that the public will realize God has truly sent him. Not everyone who gives a sign or wonder is to be accepted as a prophet. Rather, if we already knew that a person was fit for prophecy through his wisdom and deeds that raised him above others of his age, and he followed the ways of prophecy in its holiness and separation [from mundane matters], and then he came and did a sign or wonder and said that God had sent him, then it is a commandment to listen to him. It is possible that a person who performs a sign or wonder is not really a prophet but performed his wonder by means of trickery. Nevertheless, we are commanded to listen to him because he has established himself previously as a great and wise man, worthy of prophecy. We must consider him [a prophet] based on his established character.

Chapter Eight

1. The people of Israel did not believe Moses because of the signs he performed. One who believes based on signs still has doubts in his heart because the signs might have been done by means of magic or sorcery. Rather, all the signs that Moses performed in the wilderness were done based on the needs of the moment, not to serve as proofs of his prophecy.[21] At the divine Revelation at Mount Sinai, our own eyes saw [the glory of God]; our own ears heard [God's voice]. [We experienced] the fire and

(continued on page 37)

22 The faith of Israel is not based on miracles or on the testimony of Moses or any other prophet. Rather, it is based on the basis of the Revelation at Mount Sinai, which was experienced by the entire people of Israel. The Israelites witnessed the Revelation directly, so the truth of the event could not be contested. They passed on their direct testimony to the generations that came afterward, generation to generation, to our own day. It is in this sense that "we saw with our own eyes and heard with our own ears"; that is, we have received the unbroken transmission from the many thousands of Israelites who stood at Mount Sinai and experienced God's Revelation.

the voices and the flames. Moses entered into the cloud, and the voice [of God] spoke to him—but we heard. How do we know that the Revelation at Mount Sinai was the sole proof that Moses's prophecy was absolute truth? It states, "Behold I have come to you in the thickness of the cloud so that the people will hear when I speak with you and will then believe forever in your [prophecy]" (Exodus 19:9). The inference is that before this Revelation they did not totally believe [in his prophecy], but their belief was marred by doubts and afterthoughts.

3. If a prophet should arise who performs signs and great wonders, and who seeks to contradict the prophecy of Moses our teacher, we do not listen to him. We know with certainty that his signs were the result of magic and sorcery. The prophecy of Moses was not dependent on signs so that we might compare his signs to those performed by others. Rather, we saw [the Revelation of God at Mount Sinai] with our own eyes and heard with our own ears, just as Moses did.²² To what can this be compared? If witnesses gave testimony contradicting something that we ourselves saw, we surely would not listen to them and would know them to be false witnesses. The Torah teaches that we must not listen to a false prophet, even if he performs signs and wonders, because he has come to contradict that which you saw with your own eyes. Given that we believe the prophecy of Moses not because of signs he performed but because of the commandments he transmitted to us, how can we trust the sign of one who has come to contradict the prophecy of Moses—a prophecy that we ourselves saw and heard?

Chapter Nine

1. It is clear and overtly [expressed] in the Torah that the Torah's command is eternal, not subject to change, to subtraction, or to

(continued on page 39)

23 Maimonides emphasizes the eternal truth of the Torah. God gave Israel the Torah and made clear that it is not subject to revision or rejection. Anyone claiming to be a prophet who undermines the eternal truth of Torah is necessarily a false prophet.

addition. As it is stated, "All this word which I command you, you shall observe to do; you shall not add to it nor diminish from it" (Deuteronomy 13:1). It also is stated, "The revealed things are for us and our children forever so that we may do all the words of this Torah" (Deuteronomy 29:28). Thus, we have learned that we are commanded to keep all the laws of the Torah forever. No prophet is authorized to innovate anything from the time [the Torah was given]. If a person should arise, whether non-Jewish or Jewish, who performs signs or wonders, and he claims God has sent him to add or to subtract a commandment, or to explain a commandment in a manner that we did not hear from Moses; or he says the commandments that were commanded to Israel are not forever and for all generations but were only applicable for a limited time, he is a false prophet because he contradicts the prophecy of Moses. He is punishable by death by strangulation because he willfully spoke in the name of God that which he was not commanded to speak. God, blessed be He, instructed Moses that the commandments [of the Torah] are for us and our children forever; and God—unlike human beings—does not lie.[23]

2. A true prophet comes not to establish a [new] religion but to instruct the public on the words of the Torah and to warn them not to transgress, or to command them in discretionary matters [not specifically commanded in the Torah].

3. A prophet who violates his own prophecy or suppresses his prophecy is guilty of death in the eyes of Heaven. If one known to us as a prophet instructs us to violate temporarily a Torah commandment, or many commandments whether light or weighty, we are obligated to listen to him. We have learned from our early sages through tradition that [we are to listen] to

(continued on page 41)

24 The prophet Elijah sought to induce the Israelites to worship the One God and to abandon the idolatry of the Baal cult by arranging a dramatic showdown with the priests of Baal, held on Mount Carmel in the north of the land of Israel. As the people gathered to witness the spectacle, Elijah challenged the idolatrous priests to offer a sacrifice to Baal and to have Baal miraculously light the fire of the altar. The priests went through elaborate rituals—but all in vain. Baal did not produce fire for the altar. Elijah then called on God to send fire to the altar that he had erected in God's name. Although it is forbidden by Jewish law to bring sacrifices outside the Temple precincts in Jerusalem, Elijah suspended that law temporarily for the sake of sanctifying God's Name. God sent fire from heaven to light the altar. The people of Israel, upon seeing this vindication of God and the repudiation of Baal, called out that "the Lord is God, the Lord is God" (1 Kings 18). This episode provides biblical precedent for a prophet to suspend a Torah law—but only on an emergency basis and only for a limited time.

all [a prophet commands]: if he says to transgress a Torah law—as did Elijah at Mount Carmel[24]—[we are to] listen to him, with the exception being [if he commands us] to worship idols.

Chapter Ten

1. If a person worthy of receiving prophecy instructs us to serve God by fulfilling the commandments of the Torah, without adding to or subtracting from them, we do not test him by demanding that he split the sea or resurrect the dead or other such similar miracles. Rather, we say to him, "Tell us things that will happen in the future." He then does so, and we wait to see if his statements will be fulfilled. If he is wrong by only the smallest detail, this demonstrates that he is a false prophet. If every detail is fulfilled as he foretold, he should be considered by us to be a true prophet.

2. We test a would-be prophet several times. If his words are completely fulfilled, he is a true prophet.

3. Soothsayers and sorcerers predict the future. So what is the difference between a prophet and them? Soothsayers and sorcerers give imperfect predictions; some of their words are fulfilled, and some are not. It is possible that none of their words will be fulfilled.

4. If a prophet foretells bad things—for example, someone will die, or a certain year will have a famine or war—the nonfulfillment of these predictions does not negate his prophecy. The Holy One, blessed be He, is compassionate and gracious, forgiving sin; it is possible that people repented and He therefore forgave them [and withheld the predicted punishment]. But if the prophet foretells something good and it does not occur, then it is certain he is a false prophet, for God does not retract from any good that He has decreed.

✡ It is clear that the perfection of man that may truly be gloried in is the one acquired by him who has achieved, in a measure corresponding to his capacity, apprehension of Him, may He be exalted.... The way of life of such an individual, after he has achieved this apprehension, will always have in view loving-kindness, righteousness, and judgment, through assimilation to His actions, may He be exalted. (*Guide of the Perplexed* 3:54, p. 638)

☐ Laws Relating to Moral and Ethical Character

Chapter One

1. Each person has various moral dispositions; people may be quite different from one another. One is choleric, always angry. Another is serene and is not prone to anger—and if he does get angry, it is only a light anger that happens rarely. One person is very arrogant; another is exceedingly meek. One person is lustful, his soul never being completely satisfied; another is pure of heart, desiring nothing, not even the basic things needed for physical sustenance. One is greedy and cannot be satisfied with all the money in the world; another stints on himself and is satisfied with a small insufficient amount and will not strive to obtain all that he needs. One person afflicts himself with hunger, starving himself rather than grudgingly spending a penny of his own; another wastes his money profligately. So it is with other character traits: the mirthful and the melancholy, the miserly and the generous, the cruel and the merciful, the fearful and the courageous, and so forth.

2. Between every character trait and its opposite are intermediate levels of varying degrees. As to the character traits: some are innate according to one's physical nature; some are pre-dispositions, tending a person toward them more readily than to other character traits. Some are not innate but are learned from others, or are acquired through self-reflection, or are believed to be worthy of emulation.

1 One should follow the "golden mean," a balanced path that eschews extreme behavior. A Talmudic passage (Jerusalem Talmud, *Hagigah* 2:1, 77a) teaches that the way of the Torah is a narrow path; on the right is fire and on the left is snowy cold. To veer from the center road is not only misguided, it is also harmful. Maimonides elaborates on the virtues of the middle path and on the means of overcoming negative character traits in his introduction to his commentary on *Pirkei Avot* (especially chapters 4 and 5).

3.   The two extremes of each character trait are not good, and it is not appropriate for a person to adopt them or accustom himself to them. If he finds that his nature tilts to one [of the extremes] or is predisposed to one of them, or if he had already accustomed himself to one of them, he should return himself for the better and walk in the ways of the good, which is the upright way.[1]

4.   The upright way is the middle point in all character traits, equidistant from both extremes. Therefore, our early sages commanded that a person examine his character traits constantly, and evaluate them and direct them to the middle road so he will be physically sound. A person should not be choleric and quick to anger, nor like a dead person who lacks feelings. Rather, he should be in the middle, not becoming angry except for a serious matter. Likewise, a person should not lust after anything except those things that he needs for his basic sustenance, as it is stated, "A righteous person eats to satisfy his soul" (Proverbs 13:25). A person should not engage in his work except to attain that which is needed for immediate sustenance, as it is stated, "A little is good for the righteous" (Psalm 37:16). A person should not be overly stingy or profligate with his money; rather, he should give charity according to his ability and give loans appropriately to those who need [to borrow]. One should not laugh excessively or be silly, nor be overly sad and mournful. A person should maintain a constant spirit of happiness and pleasantness, with a kind countenance. So it is with the other character traits. This is the way of the sages.

2 One who generally follows the middle road is called wise. Yet, a pious person will veer a bit from the middle road so that his or her behavior will not only be proper but righteous.

5. A person whose character traits are in the middle is called wise. One who is exceedingly exacting with himself, veering a bit one way or the other from the middle path, is called pious. For example, one who distances himself to the last degree away from haughtiness, so that he is very meek, is called pious; and this is the quality of piety. If he followed the middle path so that he is humble, he is called wise; and this is the quality of wisdom.[2] And so it is with the other traits. The early pious ones would tilt their traits from the middle, sometimes toward one extreme and sometimes toward the other; this is doing more than the letter of the law requires.

3 The call to "imitate God" is understood by rabbinic tradition to refer only to God's attributes of holiness, compassion, and graciousness.

6. We are commanded to walk on the middle paths, which are good and upright, as it is stated, "And you shall walk in His ways" (Deuteronomy 28:9). Here is how [our sages] explained this commandment: just as He is called gracious, so you should be gracious; just as He is called compassionate, so you should be compassionate; just as He is called holy, so you should be holy. Our prophets described God with such adjectives as forbearing, filled with kindness, righteous and upright, pure, mighty and strong, and so forth, to teach that these are good and upright qualities that a person must adopt, emulating God as much as possible.[3]

7. How is a person to accustom himself to these qualities so that they become fixed within him? He should conduct himself according to the middle path again and yet again, and constantly repeat these behaviors until they become easy for him and do not seem a burden; these qualities will then be fixed in his soul. Because these qualities were ascribed to the Creator—that is, the middle path which we are obligated to follow—this path is known as the path of God. One who follows this path brings good and blessing to himself.

Chapter Two

1. Sick people taste the bitter as sweet and the sweet as bitter. Some desire to eat inedible foods such as dust and charcoal; they despise healthy foods such as bread and meat, each according to the gravity of the illness. So it is with people who are sick in their souls. They desire and love bad qualities, and hate the good path and are reluctant to follow it; it is very heavy to them, depending on the nature of their [spiritual] illness. What should the sick of soul do to be cured? They should go to sages, the doctors of the soul, who will cure their illnesses by guiding them in the proper qualities that will return them to the good path.

4 Although the middle path is appropriate for most traits, in several cases one should veer to an extreme. Thus, one should not only be humble but should be exceedingly humble. One should control anger to the fullest degree possible, not just to an intermediate level.

Maimonides wrote a letter to his student Joseph ben Judah after the latter had become embroiled in a controversy with Samuel ben Ali, the gaon (rabbinic leader) of Baghdad. Joseph wanted to establish an academy there in which students would study the *Mishneh Torah*, but Samuel was an opponent of Maimonides's influence. He spoke disparagingly of Maimonides and his work, and Joseph was outraged. Maimonides wrote: "If you are indeed my disciple, I want you to train yourself to follow my moral habits. The most noble conduct for you is to be reviled without reviling in turn and without letting your words get away from you" (Raymond Weiss and Charles Butterworth, *Ethical Writings of Maimonides*, p. 120).

2. What are examples of such cures? If a person is choleric, he is taught to control himself from reacting even if he is struck or cursed. He should continue in this manner for an extended period of time, until he uproots anger from his heart. If he is haughty, he should conduct himself with much self-degradation; he should sit more inconspicuously than others, dress in old tattered clothes, and similar such things until haughtiness is uprooted from him; he can then return to the middle path, which is the good path. When he then returns to the middle path, he will follow it for the rest of his life. The same method is applied to the other qualities: if a person is far to one extreme, he should distance himself to the opposite extreme and remain there for an extended period of time until he can return to the good path, which is the middle road in each quality.

3. There are some character traits for which it is forbidden to follow a middle path, but a person should go to the opposite extreme, such as with the quality of haughtiness. It is not a good path simply to be humble; a person should be meek and his spirit should be very low. Thus, it is said about Moses our teacher [that he was] "very humble" (Numbers 12:3), not just humble. So our sages commanded: one must be exceedingly meek. Likewise, the trait of anger is very bad, and it is proper for a person to accustom himself to the opposite extreme. One should teach himself not to become angry even over something worthy of inducing anger. If a person wishes to cast fear [for disciplinary reasons] over his children and household, or if he is a communal leader who wants to show anger to the community so they will return to proper behavior— [in these cases] a person should show himself to be angry for disciplinary reasons, but his internal mind should be calm so that he will be like a person pretending to be angry when he is not angry.

5   Rabbi Akiva coined the phrase "Silence is a fence around wisdom" (*Pirkei Avot* 3:13). A wise person maintains silence until he or she has something of value to say.

4. A person should accustom himself to remain silent and should avoid speaking except on matters of wisdom or on things that are necessary for one's physical needs. Even in matters of Torah and wisdom, one's words should be few but their content great.

5. Silence is a fence around wisdom.[5] Therefore, a person should not respond quickly nor speak too much. He should teach his students calmly and pleasantly, without shouting and without being verbose.

6. It is forbidden for a person to engage in slick talk and flattery. One should not say one thing with the mouth while thinking something else in the heart, but the inner and outer selves should be attuned. That which is in one's heart should correspond to that which one says with the mouth. It is forbidden to deceive people. One should not invite a friend to join for a meal when one knows that the friend cannot accept. One should not offer presents when knowing that the other will not accept them. Even one word of flattery and deception is forbidden. Rather, a person should have a true tongue, an upright spirit, and a heart pure of all deception and fraud.

7. A person should be not overly mirthful and silly, and not overly sad and and melancholy, but be happy. Our sages taught that one should receive others with a kindly countenance. A person should not be desirous of treasure, or be lazy and idle, but should be generous. One should diminish time devoted to labor so as to spend more time engaged in studying Torah. One should rejoice in what little is one's portion. A person should not be a quibbler, an envier, a luster after pleasure, or one who runs after honor.

6 The Talmud (*Taanit* 11a) quotes the opinion of the sage Samuel, who said: "One who fasts [when not required by the law to do so] is a sinner." Normative Judaism frowned on asceticism as an unnatural and unbalanced way of life. While there have been pietists and sectarians who imposed on themselves an ascetic lifestyle, Maimonides teaches that asceticism is not a religious ideal to be adopted.

Chapter Three

1.   If a person should say: Because jealousy, lust, honor, and such similar traits are the wrong path that remove a person from this world, I will separate myself from them very much and will veer to the other extreme—so that this person will not eat meat, nor drink wine, nor marry, nor live in a nice home, nor wear nice clothing but only sackcloth and coarse wool, and so forth, such as is the practice of the priests of the idolaters—this, too, is a bad path, and it is forbidden to follow it. One who follows this path is called a sinner. Our sages taught that one should not deprive oneself except of those things that the Torah has so indicated. A person should not create personal prohibitions by means of vows or oaths on things that are permissible. Our sages said, "Are you not satisfied enough with what the Torah has forbidden, that you wish to forbid yourself from other things as well?" [Jerusalem Talmud, *Nedarim* 9:53]. This includes those who constantly fast; this is not a proper path, and our sages forbade it.[6] Solomon instructed, "Be not righteous overmuch, neither make yourself overwise; why should you destroy yourself?" (Ecclesiastes 7:16).

2.   A person should direct his heart and actions entirely for the sake of knowing the Name, blessed be He. His sitting, rising, and speaking should all aim at this goal. For example, when one engages in business or works to gain income, his heart should not merely be directed toward attaining money. Rather he should see these [endeavors] as means to attain those things that the body needs, for example, food, drink, housing, and getting married. Likewise, when a person eats or drinks or engages in marital relations, he should not concentrate only on the pleasure he derives, but should have in mind that he eats and drinks only for the sake of the health of his body. A person should not eat all that his taste desires but should eat those things that are healthy for the body, whether they taste bitter or sweet. One should not eat harmful foods even if they taste sweet.

✡ The study of medicine is very important in regard to virtue, the knowledge of God, and the attainment of true happiness. To study it well is among the greatest acts of serving God. It enables us to conduct ourselves as human beings, leading us to the virtues and the truths. (*Shemonah Perakim*, chapter 5)

3. If a person follows a healthy lifestyle merely to have a healthy body and to have children who will do his work and exert themselves for his benefit, this is not a good path. Rather, one should intend that his body be healthy and strong in order that his soul will be upright to know God; for it is not possible to understand and contemplate the sciences while one is hungry and sick, or when one of the limbs is aching. One should aspire to have a child who might become a great sage in Israel. If one follows this pattern always, he thereby is constantly serving God. Even when he sleeps, if he sleeps with the idea that this will give rest to his mind and body so that he will be able to serve God in health, it turns out that his sleep [itself] is service to the Lord, blessed be He. Our sages taught that all our deeds should be for the sake of Heaven. This is what Solomon, in his wisdom, instructed: "In all your ways know Him, and He will make your paths straight" (Proverbs 3:6).

Chapter Four

1. Since maintaining a healthy and fit body is a godly way—it being impossible to understand or attain knowledge of the Creator when sick—a person must stay away from things that harm the body and must become accustomed to things that are healthful and curative. Thus, a person should not eat except when hungry, nor drink except when thirsty, nor delay an instant upon feeling the need to rid one's bodily wastes.

2. A person should not eat to the point where his stomach is full but should eat until he is three-fourths satisfied. He should only drink a little water mixed with wine during a meal. When the food begins to digest, he may drink what he wishes; but he should not drink too much water even after the food has been digested.

7 Much of chapter 4 is devoted to health guidelines advocated by Maimonides, based on the available medical knowledge of his times. While I have omitted his prescriptions relating to sleeping, eating, ridding one's wastes, cleansing, bloodletting, and engaging in marital relations, the overall theme is that the Torah teaches us to maintain our health. In modern times, this would entail such things as maintaining a healthful diet, engaging in a regular regimen of exercise, and getting enough sleep each night. It would also incorporate living a healthy and balanced lifestyle and receiving regular medical checkups.

3. A person should eat while sitting or reclining to the left. One should not walk, or ride, or exert himself, or cause his body to sweat, or travel until the food in his belly is digested. One who goes on a voyage or physically exerts himself after eating brings on himself serious and painful illnesses.

4. A day has twenty-four hours: it is enough for a person to sleep eight hours. One should sleep toward the end of the night, eight hours before dawn; at which time one should arise from bed.

20. One who follows the rules of hygiene [proper diet, cleanliness, and maintenance of good bodily habits] will not become sick until he grows old and dies, never needing a doctor. He will have a healthy and fit body all his life unless he has an innately unhealthy body, or unless he grows accustomed to bad habits from earliest childhood, or unless a plague or famine strikes him.[7]

Chapter Five

1. Just as a sage is distinguished by his wisdom and character traits, so he must be distinguished in his actions: in the way he eats, drinks, engages in marital relations, rids his wastes, speaks, walks, dresses, manages his dealings, and conducts business. All his deeds must be exceedingly pleasant and proper. Thus, a Torah scholar must not be a glutton but should only eat what his bodily health requires; he should not eat more than he needs.

2. He should eat the modest amount that he needs while in his own home, at his own table. He should not eat in a store or in the marketplace unless absolutely necessary, so as not to become depreciated in the eyes of the public. He should avoid eating the food of others except for meals connected with fulfilling a commandment, for example, a wedding feast.

✡ The following story is told about Aaron [the brother of Moses]. When he sensed or heard that a person was evil or sinful, he would greet him with alacrity, befriend him, and speak with him often. This would cause the person to be ashamed and to say to himself, "Woe unto me. If Aaron knew my inner thoughts and my [evil] deeds, he would avoid me, and certainly would not be speaking with me. Surely, he must consider me to be pious. I will [therefore] aspire to validate his opinion of me, and I will repent and become one of his students again." (Commentary on Ethics of the Fathers [Pirkei Avot] 1:12)

3. A sage drinks only enough wine to help with digestion of his meal. One who becomes intoxicated is a sinner and is despicable, and loses his wisdom. If he becomes drunk in the presence of common folk, he has thereby desecrated the Name.

4. Although marital relations are permitted, a Torah scholar should conduct himself with holiness and not be with his wife [constantly] like a rooster. He must not engage in marital relations while she is sleeping; nor may he force her if she is unwilling. Rather, this requires the willingness and happiness of both parties.

5. One who follows this practice will thereby sanctify his soul, purify himself, and regulate his character. If he has children, they will be fine and modest, worthy of wisdom and piety. One who behaves like the benighted masses will have children like those masses.

7. A Torah scholar must not shout and scream when he speaks, nor raise his voice too much; rather, his words should be pleasant when talking to everyone. He should not speak so softly as to give the impression that he is overly genteel. He should hasten to greet everyone so they will find him pleasant. He should judge others charitably, speaking in praise of others, and never disparagingly. He should love peace and pursue peace. If he sees that his words are well received and heeded, he should speak. Otherwise, he should remain silent. For example, he should not attempt to pacify someone who is having an angry outburst, nor offer consolation to one who is overwhelmed before the burial of a loved one. One should not look at someone who is in the midst of an embarrassing situation, but should raise his eyes away from that direction. In sum, one should not speak except words of wisdom or loving-kindness.

✡ If you pray merely by moving your lips while facing a wall, and at the same time think about your buying and selling; or if you read the Torah with your tongue while your heart is set upon the building of your habitation and does not consider what you read; and similarly in all cases in which you perform a commandment merely with your limbs … without reflecting either upon the meaning of that action or upon Him from whom the commandment proceeds or upon the end of the action, you should not think that you have achieved the end. Rather, you will then be similar to those of whom it is said, "Thou are near in their mouth, and far from their reins" [Jeremiah 12:2]. (*Guide of the Perplexed* 3:51, p. 622)

8. A Torah scholar must not strut around with his chin jutting out. Nor should he walk in small delicate steps like the effete. One should not run in public, as do fools. One should not bend himself over in feigned humility. One should look to the ground as though in prayer and walk as one who is busy with his work. From the way one walks, it is evident whether he is wise and proper, or foolish and vain.

9. A Torah scholar's clothes should be appropriate and clean; no dirt or stains must be found on his clothing. He should not wear luxurious clothing that will attract attention, nor should he wear shabby, disgraceful clothing. Rather, his clothes should be appropriate and of middle quality.

10. A Torah scholar manages his affairs appropriately. He provides for his family according to his means and does not overextend his expenses. Our sages taught that one should eat less than he can afford, dress according to what he can afford, and provide for his wife and children more than he can afford.

13. A Torah scholar conducts his business with integrity and honesty. He does not undermine the business of another, nor does he cause pain to others. He is patient and forgiving.

8 The Torah's commandment to love one's fellow as oneself is a lofty ideal—but how can one do this? Maimonides provides practical ways to implement this commandment based not on ethereal emotions but on realistic guidelines for human interaction. We demonstrate love for another through praise and appreciation; our words of affirmation bring joy and a sense of self-worth to the other. Likewise, our concern for the property of others is a realistic and meaningful expression of loyalty and friendship.

Chapter Six

1. It is human nature to be influenced by the attitudes and behaviors of one's neighbors and friends and to follow the mores of society. Therefore, a person should cling to the righteous and always live among sages so as to learn from their actions. One should distance himself from the wicked who walk in darkness, so as not to learn from their ways. If one lived in a realm that had bad moral traits and where the people did not walk in the upright path, he should move to a place whose residents are righteous and good. If all the lands of which he is aware have corrupt societies, or if he is unable to move to a good land due to the military situation or personal illness, then let him dwell alone. If the people around him are wicked sinners who do not let him dwell among them unless he blends in and behaves according to their bad mores, then let him exile himself to caves, thorny fields, or deserts rather than following the ways of the sinners.

3. It is a commandment to love each fellow Israelite as oneself, as it is stated, "You shall love your fellow as yourself" (Leviticus 19:18). Therefore one must speak in praise of his fellow and be concerned for his property, as one is concerned about one's own property and honor.[8] One who gains personal honor by shaming another has no place in the world to come.

9 The Torah commands us to love "the stranger," meaning non-Israelites who live within the Israelite community. This is an expression of respect for fellow human beings; everyone, regardless of ethnic background, must be treated kindly and not be made to feel as a "stranger." Rabbinic tradition interpreted the commandment to refer to people of various backgrounds who have converted to Judaism and thereby become part of the Jewish people.

The Talmud (*Bava Metzia* 59b) indicates that one who causes distress to a proselyte transgresses thirty-six commandments (some say forty-six commandments). A convert might feel vulnerable as an "outsider"; therefore, Jewish law is emphatic in protecting the rights and feelings of converts, insisting that they be treated with utmost respect and sensitivity.

4. There are two positive commandments relating to loving the proselyte who has come under the divine wings. First, he is included among those who are your fellows. Second, he is specifically [to be loved] because he is a proselyte, and the Torah states that "you shall love the stranger [proselyte]" (Deuteronomy 10:19).**9**

8. When chastising another [for having committed a sin], one should not speak harshly or cause embarrassment. A person should be careful not to shame another in public, whether a child or adult; one should not call another by a name that embarrasses him, nor should one say something to him that will cause embarrassment. These rules relate to matters between human beings; but when it comes to matters relating to [the honor of] Heaven, it is permitted to embarrass [the culprit] in public and to publicize the sin and to humiliate and curse him until he returns to the right path, just as the prophets of Israel did.

10. One must be solicitous of [the welfare of] orphans and widows because their souls are very meek and their spirits are low. This applies even if they have financial means. One should speak to them kindly and deal with them respectfully. One should not cause them physical or psychological pain.

Chapter Seven

3. Our sages taught that there are three sins for which a person is punished in this world and for which [he loses his portion] in the world to come: idolatry, sexual immorality, and murder— and evil talk is tantamount to them all! Gossip destroys three parties: the one who says it, the one who listens to it, and the one about whom it is said. The one who listens is even more culpable than the one who speaks it.

✡ When a person multiplies words, he will surely sin; it is impossible that there would not be among his words something that is not proper to say. A sign of wise men is the limiting of their words; a sign of a fool is a multitude of words.... The Sages have taught that a diminution of words is evidence of the nobility of one's parents and of the person's pure lineage. (Commentary on *Ethics of the Fathers* [*Pirkei Avot*] 1:17)

4.   There are things that are akin to outright gossip: for example [if a person says], "Who would have known that X would have been in the current situation," or "Be quiet about X; I don't want to tell you what happened to him," or similar such phrases [that plant negative thoughts into the hearts of the listeners]. One should not praise a person in the presence of his enemies, because this also is akin to gossip, causing [the enemies to respond] and speak negatively.

7.   One who takes revenge transgresses a negative commandment, as it is stated, "You shall not take revenge" (Leviticus 19:18). It is proper for a person to be forgiving, because wise people understand that matters of this world are vain and empty—not worthy of taking revenge over. What is an example of taking revenge? If one asked to borrow a neighbor's axe, and the neighbor refused; and the next day, the neighbor asked to borrow his axe, and he replied, "I will not lend to you just as you did not lend to me." This is revenge. Rather, if the neighbor comes to borrow, you should lend with a full heart and not do unto him as he did to you.

8.   Likewise, one who bears a grudge transgresses a negative commandment, as it is stated, "You shall not bear a grudge against one of your people" (Leviticus 19:18). What is an example of bearing a grudge? Reuben requested of Simon, "Rent me this house or lend me this ox," and Simon refused. Later, Simon came to Reuben to borrow or rent from him. Reuben replied, "Here, take it. I am lending to you, unlike what you did [to me]; I will not act to you according to your behavior [to me]." This is bearing a grudge. The Torah was insistent that one should not bear a grudge or remember past misdeeds [committed against him]. This [spirit of forgiveness] is the proper moral trait that can sustain society and interpersonal relations.

1 Talmudic law obligated fathers to ensure that their sons were instructed in Torah. This reflected the prevalent societal assumptions of those times, that boys had the intellectual capacity and social responsibility to become educated. It was widely thought that girls lacked intellectual capacity and, in any case, did not require much education outside of what they could learn from their mothers. Maimonides generally accepted these assumptions; he describes the obligation of Torah study as applying to males.

During the twentieth century, great rabbinic authorities saw the need to update the Talmudic and medieval assumptions, allowing and even encouraging full educational opportunities, including Torah education, for girls and women. Thus, a vast network of Jewish day schools developed in which girls and boys have been receiving a thorough religious and general education. Under the direction of Rabbi Joseph B. Soloveitchik, the preeminent rabbinic authority of modern Orthodoxy in the United States, girls and women have been provided serious opportunities to study Torah, including Talmud and halakhic literature.

2 Teaching Torah is a high obligation and privilege. It is praiseworthy to teach children who might otherwise not receive Torah education, especially children of the poor. A Talmudic adage states, "Be mindful of the children of the poor, because from them will the Torah go forth" (*Nedarim* 81a).

3 From the first stages in children's intellectual development, they are to be taught fundamental principles of Judaism. Children learn that the Torah of Moses is an inheritance of the Jewish people. Thus, their lives are put into the contexts of Torah and Jewish peoplehood. Children also learn to recite the *Sh'ma,* the quintessential Jewish affirmation of the unity of God. These concepts, taught at the youngest possible age, serve as spiritual foundations that remain with the children as they grow and mature.

☐ Laws of Torah Study

Chapter One

2. Just as a man is obligated to teach his son,[1] so he is obligated to teach his grandson. [The obligation to teach Torah applies] not only to one's son and grandson; each sage in Israel [is obligated] to teach all students even if they are not his children.[2]

3. One whose father did not teach him Torah is obligated to teach himself when he is old enough to understand.

6. When is a father obligated to begin teaching his son Torah? As soon as the child begins to speak, the father teaches him "Moses commanded us the Torah" and the first verse of the Sh'ma.[3] Afterward, he teaches little by little, verse by verse, until the child is six or seven years old, depending on the child's abilities; then he brings the child to study with a teacher.

4 The Torah belongs to the entire Jewish people, and all have access to it. We are instructed to study Torah day and night to the extent of our ability, so that we become well versed in its teachings and come to feel familiar with its words. The Torah is not the exclusive preserve of a priestly or scholarly class, but the inheritance of all the people.

It has been customary since antiquity for portions of the Torah to be read publicly on Monday and Thursday mornings, as well as on the morning and afternoon of the Sabbath. The prevalent custom in most Jewish communities is to read a portion of the Torah at the synagogue services on each Sabbath morning, so that the entire Torah is completed during the course of one year. Those who attend services regularly will thereby gain familiarity with the entire Torah. It is also a long-standing custom for rabbis to provide insights into the Torah portion of each week, either through classes or sermons.

5 Maimonides points to the greatness of Talmudic sages who worked for a living, even at menial jobs. They considered it a virtue to earn their income without depending on charity. By engaging in labor, scholars not only maintained their independence and self-respect, but they also gained a clearer understanding of the realities of economic life that confronted all other members of the community. Their understanding of Torah was enhanced by their understanding of life, and they could teach with greater wisdom and sensitivity.

8.   Each Jewish man is obligated to study Torah, whether poor or rich, whether healthy or afflicted, whether young or very old and of weakened strength. Even a poor person who is sustained by charity and goes begging from door to door, even a man with wife and children—each must set aside time each day and night to study Torah.[4]

9.   Among the great Jewish sages were hewers of wood and drawers of water and blind men; nevertheless they engaged in Torah study during the day and at night. They are among the transmitters of our tradition, from person to person going back to Moses our teacher.[5]

6 The word *talmud* literally means "study" or "analysis." While the Written Torah and the Oral Torah are foundations of religious knowledge, it is incumbent on the student to go beyond simple rote learning. Once the basic sources have been mastered, one then should advance to careful analysis of the texts to seek deeper meanings, to detect and resolve apparent contradictions, and to determine how to apply the sources to new situations. As noted earlier, the Written Torah refers to the Five Books of Moses. The Oral Torah refers to the Mishnah and other early rabbinic traditions relating to the interpretation of the Written Torah. The Talmud includes the laws of the Mishnah but is primarily composed of the Gemara—a collection of discussions of the teachings of the Mishnah, legal arguments, and rigorous analyses.

Aside from the legal content of the Talmud, there is a substantial and significant body of literature known as "Aggadah" (homilies). The Aggadah, which contains stories, parables, folklore, and ethical insights, is intermixed with the legal discussions of the Gemara.

7 As pointed out earlier ("Foundations of the Torah" 4:13), "the Orchard" refers to metaphysical speculation. It also is applied to the study of Kabbalah, Jewish mysticism.

11. A person must divide his study time into three parts: one-third in the Written Torah, one-third in the Oral Torah, and one-third in intellectual analysis and inductions, deriving and comparing one thing to another. This latter is known as Talmud.[6]

12. The Holy Scriptures are included in the [category of] Written Torah, and their commentaries are included in the Oral Torah. Topics known as the Orchard are in the category of intellectual analysis.[7] The [threefold division of study time] applies in one's early stages of study. However, when one grows in wisdom, one will not need to study the Written Torah or the Oral Torah. He can read them at set times so as not to forget any of the laws of the Torah; but he should devote all his days to Talmud alone, according to his inclination and ability to concentrate.

8 Maimonides's ruling against teaching Talmud to girls and women, which derives from the opinion of Rabbi Eliezer (*Sotah* 20a), is based on the belief that most women do not have the intellectual capacity to handle the complexities of halakhic analysis. Rabbi Haim David Halevy (1924–1998), for many years the Sephardic chief rabbi of Tel Aviv, suggested that in olden times, girls received no formal education at all; thus, learning Talmud would have been far beyond their grasp. They simply lacked the rudimentary training to be prepared for analysis of Talmud. Since in modern times girls do receive formal education and demonstrate intellectual talents in so many areas of study, they may also be taught Talmud (*Mayyim Hayyim* 2:89).

Maimonides recognized that women could indeed achieve the highest levels of intellectual perfection. He was well aware of examples of women prophets in the Bible. In his view, a person could not become a prophet without first being a philosopher; thus, the Bible itself provides proof that women can—and did—reach great intellectual heights. Moreover, Maimonides's first chapters of the *Mishneh Torah* deal with the commandments to know, love, and fear God; these commandments are applicable to women as well as men. Yet, for Maimonides, the fulfillment of these commandments presupposes a prior knowledge of physics and metaphysics. The clear implication is that women have the basic intellectual talents to fulfill these commandments; otherwise, they would have been exempted from them.

9 A hallmark of Jewish life since antiquity has been the emphasis on education. The Talmud credits Rabbi Joshua ben Gamla (first century CE) with having established an educational system that provided instruction for all children, rich and poor. His plan required each community to appoint teachers to educate the children. "May Rabbi Joshua ben Gamla be remembered for the good; if not for him, the Torah would have been forgotten from Israel" (*Bava Batra* 21a).

13. A woman who studies Torah receives reward, but not to the same extent as a man, because she was not commanded [to study Torah].[8]

Chapter Two

1. Teachers are appointed in each country, in each county, and in each city.[9] The world only exists by virtue of the breath of children studying Torah.

Chapter Three

1. Israel was crowned with three crowns: the crown of Torah, the crown of priesthood, and the crown of kingship. The crown of priesthood was merited by Aaron; the crown of kingship was merited by David. The crown of Torah stands ready and available for every Jew; anyone who wishes may come and claim it. The crown of Torah is greater than the other two crowns.

3. Among all the commandments, none is equal to the study of Torah. Study leads to proper action.

10 The ideal is to study Torah without thought of reward in either this world or the world to come. Study of Torah should be for its own sake, for the pursuit of knowledge of God and His ways. Not everyone can reach this level of commitment without previous preparation. In his introduction to *Perek Helek,* Maimonides points out that a child needs to be promised rewards as an encouragement to study. As the child grows older, the rewards become greater. At some point, though, the child will come to realize that study is valuable in its own right, at which point external rewards are no longer needed. That is the goal to which everyone should aspire.

However, if a person has not reached this lofty level of pure study, he or she should still engage in Torah study, even if not for its own sake, to gain merit in this world and in the world to come. Although this is a childlike attitude, the Talmud teaches that it will ultimately lead one to develop a more mature and idealistic approach to Torah study (*Pesahim* 50b).

11 Maimonides draws on a teaching found in *Ethics of Our Fathers* (*Pirkei Avot)* 2:5. This does not mean that one should not engage in business activities; only that one should not be so overly consumed with business that no time or energy is left for Torah study. A person should see Torah as the central focus of life, while business is the means to provide the economic wherewithal to enable one to engage in Torah study to the extent possible.

5.   [In the world to come] a person's judgment begins with [how he dealt with the commandment to] study Torah. Therefore our sages said: a person should engage in Torah study whether for its own sake or not for its own sake, since by means of Torah study even not for its own sake, one will come to study it for its own sake.**10**

6.   To properly fulfill the commandment of Torah study and to earn the crown of Torah, one should not be distracted by other matters. He should not set his heart on acquiring Torah as well as wealth and honor. The reward is in proportion to the exertion.

7.   If one should say, "Once I've accumulated wealth I will return to the study of Torah" or "Once I acquire what I need, I will then leave off my work"—if this kind of thinking enters your heart, you will never merit the crown of Torah. Rather, you must make the Torah your fixed duty, and your work should be subservient. Do not say, "When I have time I will study," for perhaps you will not have time.

8.   It is written in the Torah that it [the Torah] is not in heaven nor across the sea (Deuteronomy 30:12–13). [This verse is interpreted to mean] that it is not found among the haughty nor among those who travel [excessively for business]. Our sages taught that one who overly engages in business does not grow wise; the sages instructed that one minimize business so as to engage more in Torah study.**11**

12 Maimonides is a powerful and eloquent voice calling for students of Torah to earn a living and not be dependent on charity for their sustenance. When rabbinical students and scholars are viewed by the public as charity cases who live parasitical existences, this causes disgrace to the Torah way of life. Moreover, those who refuse to work at gainful employment, preferring to live on the charitable handouts of others, eventually may find themselves in dire economic straits. Thus, they may come to steal and cheat to sustain themselves and their families. This leads to a profound desecration of God's Name. People will say, "If Torah scholars steal and cheat, what is the value of Torah?" By participating honestly and constructively in the social and economic fabric of the community, Torah scholars not only maintain their own self-respect, but win the respect of others.

10. Anyone who decides to study Torah and not work [for a living] but live off of charity desecrates the Name and disgraces the Torah and extinguishes the light of religion. He causes evil to himself and deprives himself of the world to come because it is forbidden to gain this-worldly benefit from Torah. All Torah that is not accompanied by work is ultimately annulled and leads to sin. The end of such a person [who studies but does not work] is that he will steal from others [to sustain himself].**12**

11. It is a high virtue to support oneself through one's own work; this was the characteristic of the early pious ones. In this way, a person merits all the honor and good of this world and the world to come.

13 Torah study is enhanced when one stays focused on the text. Studying in a synagogue or study hall, in the midst of others who are also studying Torah, is beneficial; one is stimulated by the general atmosphere created by groups of people engaged in Torah study.

One must concentrate when reading. A quick skimming of a text will yield poorer results than a careful, analytical reading. Maimonides suggests techniques that help one to study more and study better. One should study quietly and modestly, trying to stay absorbed in the text. One should study Torah in a soft, audible voice, rather than reading only in one's mind or in a whisper. Saying the words aloud helps one to remember them better. Unless one is able to verbalize the meaning of the text, one may not fully understand it.

12. Our sages said, "It is a sure covenant that one who exerts himself to study Torah in the synagogue will not soon forget [that which he learns]." One who exerts himself in study in an inconspicuous way will grow wise. One who can hear his own voice as he studies—his study will remain with him; but one who reads in a whisper will soon forget.[13]

13. Although it is a commandment to study Torah during the day and at night, a person gains most of his wisdom only at night. One who wishes to merit the crown of Torah should be careful not to waste even one night in sleeping, eating, drinking, chattering, and so forth. Rather [one should devote himself to] Torah and matters of wisdom.

Chapter Four

4. If a teacher taught but the students did not understand, the teacher should not become angry at them. Rather, he should review and repeat the matter even several times until they understand the depth of the law. A student should not say "I understand" when in fact he has not understood, but he should continue to ask even a number of times. If his teacher becomes angry, he should say, "Rabbi, it is Torah and I must learn it, and my understanding is limited."

5. A student should not be embarrassed that his classmates learned something the first or second time, and he did not learn except after a number of times. If he is embarrassed by this, he will have entered and left the study hall without having learned anything.

[14] Rabbinic tradition has long emphasized the importance of a strong teacher-student relationship. A Torah teacher must be patient and respectful to students and must be genuinely devoted to them. Teaching Torah is a holy obligation and privilege. It entails the transmission not only of information and learning skills, but also of spiritual, moral, and emotional content. The teacher must be a role model from whom students can experience the positive qualities of religion.

Jewish law formulated various rules to enhance the status of Torah teachers in the eyes of their students. For example, students are to rise respectfully when their Torah teacher enters the room. They are always to address their teacher deferentially. They are not to refer to their teacher in a casual way, or to address the teacher by his first name. These formal rules were intended to foster a proper and respectful relationship, so that students looked upon teachers with reverence.

Chapter Five

1. Just as a person is commanded to honor and fear his father, so he is obligated to honor and fear his teacher—the teacher even more so than the father. The father has brought him into this world, while the teacher who imparts wisdom leads him to the world to come.

4. Any student who has not achieved the knowledge to teach Torah law and yet does so is foolish, wicked, and arrogant. On the other hand, a student who has achieved the knowledge to teach Torah law and yet does not do so withholds Torah and puts obstacles before the blind [by not clarifying the laws for the public, thus causing them to continue to walk in darkness]. Inadequately trained students, who have not learned enough Torah, seek to aggrandize themselves among the ignorant and townsfolk. They are quick to sit at the head to judge and teach. They increase controversy, destroy the world, extinguish the light of Torah, and trample the vineyard of the Lord of Hosts.

5. It is forbidden for a student to call his rabbi by his name, even when not in his presence. One should not greet or return greetings from his rabbi in the same manner as he would do with friends. Rather, he should bow his head before the rabbi and say with fear and respect, "Peace upon you, Rabbi." If the rabbi had greeted him first, he should reply, "Peace upon you, my rabbi and teacher."[14]

10. Every rabbinic scholar with upright qualities does not speak in the presence of one who is wiser, even if he had not learned anything from him.

15 Although teachers are to be highly respected by their students, it is also essential for teachers to be respectful of their students. The Talmud cites the opinion of Rabbi Elazar ben Shamua: "Let the honor of your student be as dear to you as your own; let the honor of your peer be as dear to you as the reverence of your rabbi; and let the reverence of your rabbi be as the reverence of Heaven" (*Pirkei Avot* 4:12).

16 Maimonides here cites the statement of Rabbi Hanina (*Taanit* 7a). This statement is part of a Talmudic discussion stressing that greater scholars need to be receptive to what they can learn from lesser scholars. Scholars are sharpened by the give-and-take of the learning process. When their opinions are challenged or questioned—even by lesser scholars, and even by students—they are forced to rethink their statements, defend them, or revise them. The learning process is dynamic, and all participants play a role in advancing knowledge. Rabbi Hanina's statement reflects the fact that alert, questioning students sharpen the minds of their teachers. The teachers must prepare their lessons carefully and must be welcoming of questions they may not have anticipated. A teacher who has learned much from students is a good teacher, and it can be assumed that the students have learned much from such a teacher.

12. Just as students are obligated to honor the rabbi, so the rabbi must honor his students and encourage them. Our sages taught, "Let the honor of your student be as dear to you as your own."[15]

13. Students increase the wisdom of their teachers and expand their understanding. Our sages said, "Much wisdom have I learned from my teachers, and more from my friends, and most from my students."[16]

Chapter Six

1. It is a commandment to honor every rabbinic scholar, even one who is not one's own teacher.

3. It is not proper for a rabbinic scholar to burden the public by purposely going past them so that they will [be required] to stand up before him [in order to show honor]. Rather he should walk by the shortest route and try not to be seen by them, so as not to cause them to stand.

9. One stands in honor of a very elderly person, even one who is not a sage. A young sage should stand in honor of a very elderly person. He need not stand upright but only enough to show honor. One should honor the elderly with kind words and by giving a hand to support them. It is stated, "One must stand in the presence of the aged" (Leviticus 19:32); this refers to all elderly people, whether Jewish or non-Jewish.

1 Anthropologists have posited that primitive humans were polytheists and idolaters who worshipped heavenly orbs or the powers of nature. As humans became more sophisticated, they gradually moved toward the belief in one God. Maimonides offers a very different view, based on his reading of the Torah.

The Torah begins with the account of God's creation of the world, culminating with the creation of Adam and Eve. The first human beings had direct dialogue with God. Surely, they were monotheists who had firsthand knowledge of God. Since humanity began with clear and direct knowledge of God, how did idolatry emerge?

Idolatry was a regression for humanity. It arose not due to denial of the One God, but due to religious errors about how to worship God. People came to think that it was appropriate to worship the sun or other heavenly orbs not because these things had innate divinity but because they were honored creations of the One God. By showing reverence to these creations of God, they thought they were actually showing reverence to God. Once they grew accustomed to worshipping God's creations, though, they gradually slipped into idolatry, and they began to believe that these creations actually had divine powers or that idols were symbols of divine powers. They then lapsed into total idolatry, so that the clear and direct knowledge of the One God was nearly lost among humanity. The question then became: How could humanity return to its original relationship with the One God?

☐ Laws of Idolatry

Chapter One

1. In the days of Enosh [son of Seth and grandson of Adam],
    human beings made a great error, and the thoughts of the
    sages of that generation became corrupted. Enosh himself was
    among those who erred. This was their mistake. They said,
    "Because God created the stars and heavenly spheres to
    govern the world, placing them on high with honor as His
    servants, then it is proper to praise and exalt and revere them.
    It must be the will of God, blessed be He, that we aggrandize
    and honor that which He has aggrandized and honored, just
    as a king would want us to honor his high-ranking servants—
    this is the honor of the king." Once this thought entered their
    hearts, they began to build altars to the stars and to sacrifice
    offerings to them, and to praise and exalt them with words and
    to bow to them, thinking erroneously that this would find
    favor with the Creator. This was the basis of idolatry, and this
    is how the idolaters who understood its basis explained it.
    They did not say, "There is no god other than this star." Rather,
    their error and foolishness was that they imagined that this
    nonsense [of serving stars] was God's will.[1]

✡ Righteous people speak little but do much. For example, Abraham our father promised [three angelic visitors] a loaf of bread; yet he served them butter, milk, a calf, and three cakes made of fine flour. In contrast, the wicked make large promises, but do nothing. For example, Efron said much [that he would give Abraham a burial place for Sarah, at no cost]; yet in fact he did not forgo even one bit of [the field's] worth [but charged full price]. (Commentary on *Ethics of the Fathers* [*Pirkei Avot*] 1:14)

2.   With the passage of time, false prophets arose and said that God commanded, "Worship a certain star or all the stars, and bring certain offerings and libations. Build an altar and make an image so all the people can bow to it." [The false prophet] informed them to fashion an idol and said that this image of the star, which he concocted from his own imagination, was transmitted to him through prophecy. In this way, they began to make idols in their temples, under trees, atop mountains, and in the valleys; they gathered the people together to bow to them. [The false prophets] told the people that the idol brings good and evil, and that it is proper to serve it and fear it. The priests [of idolatry] said, "By performing this service, you will multiply and succeed; do this but do not do that." Then other false prophets arose and claimed that a star or an angel spoke to them and instructed them, "Worship me in such and such a manner." And they informed of the manner of worship, what to do and what not to do. This spread so that the entire world came to serve idols with various types of service, each different from the other, and to bring offerings and to bow [to them]. With the passage of time, the honored and awesome Name was forgotten among all people and from their minds, and they did not recognize Him. Consequently, the masses of people only knew idols of wood or stone, and altars of stones. From their childhoods, they had been taught to bow to [their idol], to serve it, and to swear in its name. The wise among them, such as the priests, gave the impression that there was no god other than the stars and heavenly spheres whose images were represented in the idols. But the Rock of the universe—no one recognized Him, and only a few individuals in the world knew Him, such as Methuselah, Noah, Shem, and Ever. In this way did the world regress until the birth of the foundation of the world—Abraham our father.

2 Maimonides's account of the theological strivings of Abraham is largely based on ancient rabbinic homilies known as Midrash. The biblical text itself provides no information about how Abraham came into a relationship with God.

Maimonides cites two different midrashic traditions that seem to be in conflict with each other. One tradition has it that Abraham was only a young child when he reasoned that there must be a God who created the universe. This underscores the amazing, even miraculous, precociousness of Abraham. The other tradition suggests that Abraham was forty years old (or more) when he discovered God. This points to Abraham's discovering God through mature philosophical speculation.

Maimonides adopts both of these traditions. He explains that Abraham was just a child when he had his first inklings about God. But it was not until he was forty years old that he actually "recognized his Creator." A child might have important preliminary insights, but only a mature philosopher can achieve true recognition of God.

3.   Once this mighty one [Abraham] was weaned, while still a child, he began to reflect and ponder day and night. He was perplexed: How is it possible for the heavenly sphere to operate constantly without there being one to direct it? Who rotates it? It is impossible for it to rotate on its own! He had no teacher and no informant, but was entrenched in Ur Kasdim among foolish idolaters. His father and mother and the entire population were idolaters, and he worshipped among them, too. But his heart reflected and understood, until he attained the true way and comprehended the just line [of thought] through his own clear understanding. He knew there is One God, and it is He who directs the heavenly sphere and who created everything. There is no God other than He. [Abraham] realized that everyone was mistaken and understood how they had fallen into their error; that is, they worshipped stars and idols until they lost the truth from their minds. At age forty, Abraham recognized his Creator.[2] Once he recognized and understood [that there is only One God], he began to ask questions to the residents of Ur Kasdim and to argue with them. He said, "You are not following the true path." He shattered idols and explained to the people that it is only fitting to worship One God. Only to Him was it proper to pray, and to make offerings and libations, so that all future generations will recognize Him. [He told them that] it was appropriate to destroy and shatter all the idols so that people will not fall into the error of imagining there is no God other than these [idols].

(continued on page 95)

3 According to the Midrash, King Nimrod was outraged by Abraham's causing spiritual turmoil among the populace. Nimrod wanted to maintain the tranquility of the status quo, where he—and not a mysterious, invisible God—was in charge. Nimrod had Abraham arrested and cast him into a fiery furnace. Miraculously, Abraham was not hurt; he managed to escape to Haran, where he continued on his way to the land of Canaan. This midrashic tale was no doubt influenced by the story from chapter 3 of the book of Daniel, where Nebuchadnezzar had Hananyah, Mishael, and Azaryah cast into a fiery furnace because they refused to worship an idol. Just as these heroes of faith were saved by God's miracle, so Abraham was saved by God. Abraham's voice could not be silenced by Nimrod. Abraham would continue his career, seeking to return humanity to its pristine original relationship with the One God.

When he overcame them with his proofs, the king [Nimrod] wanted to murder him, but a miracle [saved Abraham] and he fled to Haran.[3] He began to call out in a loud voice to all the world, and to inform them that there is but One God in the universe and it is proper to serve Him. He traveled from town to town and from kingdom to kingdom, calling out and gathering the public, until he reached the land of Canaan, where he proclaimed [God], as it states, "And he called there in the name of God, Lord of the universe" (Genesis 21:33). When people gathered around him and asked him about his teachings, he explained to each one according to his level of understanding until he returned him to the true path. Thousands and tens of thousands gathered around Abraham and became members of the house of Abraham. He planted in their hearts this great principle [of One God], and he wrote books, and he communicated this [wisdom] to his son Isaac. Isaac taught and reviewed [these teachings to the public], and transmitted them to Jacob, whom [Isaac] appointed to be teacher; and [Jacob] taught and reviewed to all who joined him. Jacob taught his sons and appointed Levi as [spiritual] head, and settled him in a school to teach the ways of the Name and to follow the commandments of Abraham. He instructed his sons that the family of Levi, generation after generation, should always be appointed to this role so that the teachings will never be forgotten. This process continued and grew stronger among the children of Jacob and those who joined them, so that a nation was formed in the world which knew God. When the Israelites spent a long period in Egypt [as slaves], they regressed; they learned to worship idols as [did the Egyptians]. Only the tribe of Levi maintained the commandment of their forefathers and never worshipped idols.

(continued on page 97)

✡ It is manifest that all of [the laws forbidding idolatry] have in view deliverance from the errors of idolatry and from other incorrect opinions that may accompany idolatry, such as belief in soothsayers, enchanters, sorcerers, charmers, and others belonging to the same group.... In order to keep people away from all magical practices, it has been prohibited to observe any of their usages, even those attaching to agricultural and pastoral activities and other activities of the kind. (*Guide of the Perplexed* 3:37, pp. 540, 543)

In a short time, it could have transpired that the faith planted by Abraham would have been uprooted, and the children of Jacob would have reverted to the errors and perversities of the [idolatrous] nations. Because of God's love of us, and His keeping the promise He had made to Abraham our father, he appointed Moses our teacher and teacher of all prophets and sent him [to redeem us]. Once Moses our teacher was endowed with prophecy and God chose Israel as His inheritance, He crowned them with commandments and informed them of the way to serve Him. He told them what would be the judgment of idolaters and all who erred [after idolatry].

Chapter Two

1. The essential commandment relating to idolatry is not to serve any created thing—not an angel, not a heavenly sphere, not a star, not one of the four elements, and not anything made from them. Even if the idolater knows that God is the Lord and intends to worship the created thing in the same way that Enosh and his generation originally did, this constitutes idolatry.

2. Idolatrous authors have composed many books about their forms of worship, describing the essential practices and rules of their service. The Holy One, blessed be He, commanded us not to read such books at all and not to think about them or the topics they discuss. Even to look at the form of an idol is forbidden. One should not inquire about the form of [idolatrous] service even if one does not worship it, because this leads one to follow after it and to do what the others do.

4 Maimonides recognized that most people are not sophisticated philosophers. While he believed it essential for all people to know basic philosophical and theological truths, he did not think they could safely handle highly abstruse speculation. If they read heretical works or entertained idolatrous thoughts, many would be negatively influenced. Their faith in the One God would be weakened or altogether undermined. Maimonides promoted intellectual striving but cautioned that this striving should stay within the boundaries of one's capacity. Maimonides feared that those with a smattering of knowledge would tend to speculate on matters beyond their ken. He was concerned such people might develop mistaken ideas and then go on to influence others with these incorrect notions. Maimonides wanted to allow people enough freedom to think and speculate, but not enough freedom to endanger themselves and others.

5 One's knowledge of God should be entirely free of idolatrous aspects. Not only is it forbidden to worship false gods; it is forbidden even to verbally admit the validity of idolatry.

3.   Not only is it forbidden to turn after idolatrous thoughts, but we are warned not to entertain any thought that may lead to the uprooting of a principle of the Torah. We should not lose focus on this, lest we follow after the [idolatrous] inclinations of the heart. Human understanding is limited, and not every mind is able to attain the truth in its purity. If one follows the inclinations of the heart, it may result in the undermining of the world due to one's limited understanding.[4]

4.   One who admits the validity of idolatry thereby denies the entire Torah, all the prophets, and all the commandments transmitted to the prophets from Adam to the end of time. One who denies idolatry thereby admits the validity of the entire Torah, all the prophets, and all the commandments transmitted to the prophets from Adam to the end of time.

6.   One who admits to the validity of idolatry, even if he did not worship it, disgraces and blasphemes the honored and awesome Name.[5] Both an idolater and a blasphemer deny the fundamental principle [of faith in God].

6   Judaism demands recognition of One God and is adamant in its rejection of all forms of idolatry. It forbids worship or veneration of anything other than God. Superstition arises among ignorant and misguided individuals who seek to manipulate God to ward off evil or to achieve some desired goal. Superstition is akin to idolatry in that both recognize supernatural powers other than, or more powerful than, God.

Maimonides insisted on a clear boundary line between true religion and superstition. He was highly critical of those individuals—even those who were seemingly religious believers in God—who resorted to superstitious beliefs and practices. For example, an individual who whispers a charm or reads a biblical verse over a wound, thinking that this incantation will effect a cure, has "repudiated the Torah." The person may think he or she is being pious by chanting a verse from the holy Bible; however, Maimonides considers this person, or those who use Torah scrolls or other sacred objects as magical utensils, to be in the category of sorcerers and charmers. They utilize religious words or artifacts as though they have independent power, which is not true religion but superstition. However, it is permissible for a healthy person to chant verses from the Bible in the hope that this will protect from affliction because the reader is not attributing intrinsic supernatural powers to the biblical words. The reading of these verses, in a sense, serves the function of prayer: it is directed to the One God, who has the power to protect.

Maimonides's sharp critique of superstitious belief and practices was not—and is not—shared by all rabbis. His opponents could point to numerous examples in the Talmud where the ancient sages believed in charms, amulets, and demons. If the Talmudic sages believed in these things, then they must be true! To this day, there are "holy" men and women who claim to perform miraculous cures, who write magical amulets, who bless food or water so as to make them efficacious for healing illnesses, and so forth. Maimonides's powerful efforts to purge superstition from religion has not met with full success. The folk spirit has not given up its attachment to superstitious ways of manipulating God through the employment of magical powers.

Chapter Eleven

2. If one whispers an incantation on a wound [to heal it] and recites a verse from the Torah; or recites a verse over a child to alleviate its fright; or places a Torah scroll or tefillin on a child to enable it to sleep—not only are such people in the category of sorcerers and soothsayers, but they are included among those who deny the Torah. They use the Torah's words as bodily cures, whereas they are for the health of the soul. But a healthy person who reads [biblical] verses or a psalm with the idea that the merit of reading them will protect from sufferings and damages—this is permissible.[6]

14. It is forbidden to consult with one who calls up ghosts or spirits, as it is stated, "There shall not be found among you any one who makes his son or daughter pass through the fire, one that uses divination, a soothsayer, an enchanter, a sorcerer, or a charmer, or one who consults a ghost or a familiar spirit, or a necromancer" (Deuteronomy 18:10–11).

7 The Torah forbade turning to sorcerers and charmers to solve our problems. Rather, we should turn directly to God with our prayers. Maimonides makes clear that sorcerers and charmers are fraudulent; they do not possess the perfect supernatural powers that they claim for themselves. Going to them is incorrect religiously and practically.

The Torah's command that we be "wholehearted with the Lord your God" was taken by Maimonides as a foundation for proper religious life. If we are "wholehearted" with God, we will not turn to other gods; we will not consult sorcerers and charmers; we will not resort to superstitious practices. We will stay focused on God alone, in a pure and trusting faith.

16. These things are all false and deceptive. Through these means did the ancient idolaters mislead the nations of the world. It is not fitting for Israelites, who are exceedingly wise, to follow after these vanities, nor to imagine that there is any value in them. As it is stated, "For there is no enchantment for Jacob, nor any divination with Israel" (Numbers 23:23). Anyone who believes in such things and imagines them to contain truth and wisdom, but believes that they are prohibited by the Torah [in spite of their efficacy] is among the fools and the deficient in understanding. People of wisdom and pure understanding know through clear proofs that these things prohibited by the Torah are not matters of wisdom but are empty and vain, having attracted to them those of deficient understanding who cast aside all the ways of truth because of them. The Torah has warned us about all these vanities: "Be wholehearted with the Lord your God" (Deuteronomy 18:13).[7]

1 The verbal confession mentions sins, transgressions, and trespasses. "Sins" refers to wrongful deeds committed unintentionally or without realizing that they were sinful. "Transgressions" refers to wrongful deeds committed intentionally. "Trespasses" refers to wrongful deeds committed intentionally and spitefully. Aside from these generic categories, one must enumerate his or her specific misdeeds. The verbal confession must be accompanied by a spirit of genuine contrition and a resolve toward future improvement.

☐ Laws of Repentance

Chapter One

1. One who transgresses any positive or negative commandment of the Torah, whether intentionally or unwittingly, must confess before God when repenting and turning from sin. This entails verbal confession; it is a positive commandment to confess [one's sins]. How does one confess? One says: "Please God! I have sinned, I have transgressed, I have trespassed[1] before You and have done such and such; behold, I am regretful and ashamed of my deed, and I will never repeat it." This is the essence of confession. One who increases confessions and elaborates [on one's sins]—he is to be praised.

2 | In ancient Israel, people could bring offerings to the Temple in Jerusalem as part of the atonement process. The Temple service was a vivid, experiential way for a sinner to purify the soul from sin and to strengthen the relationship with God. The First Temple, built during the reign of King Solomon, was razed by the Babylonians in 586 BCE. The Second Temple, dedicated in 516 BCE, was destroyed by the Romans in 70 CE. The two Temples spanned a period of one thousand years of operation and served as central foci of the religious life of Israel. The destruction of the First Temple brought great despair to the Israelites; but within a seventy-year period, they were successful in building the Second Temple. However, following the destruction of the Second Temple, Jewish sovereignty in the Holy Land came to an end—until the State of Israel was declared in 1948. There was no possibility over these many centuries to build a Third Temple; even now, with a reestablished Jewish state in the Land of Israel, it is not too conceivable that such a Temple will be built in the near future.

Once the Temple service was removed as a factor in atonement for sins, how then were Jews to purify their souls? The classic answer of the prophets and sages was that in place of the Temple ritual, we have prayer; in place of the atonement offerings, we have repentance.

3 | Once a year, on the Day of Atonement, Jews come before the Almighty to repent their sins and seek forgiveness. In Temple days, the Day of Atonement was marked by elaborate rituals. This was the only day of the year when the High Priest entered the room in the Temple known as the Holy of Holies, where he prayed on behalf of the people of Israel. Since the destruction of the ancient Temples, the Day of Atonement has been marked by solemn prayers in synagogues. The traditional liturgy of the Day of Atonement synagogue service includes a description of the services that once took place in the Temples in ancient Jerusalem.

The Day of Atonement is considered to have intrinsic holiness, with the power to cleanse sinners of their sins. Atonement is for sins committed against God, that is, violations of religious ritual laws such as desecration of the Sabbath or eating forbidden foods. Yet, Maimonides notes that atonement is not automatic; rather, it is granted only to those who sincerely repent.

3.   In our times, when the Temple does not exist and we do not have access to the altar of atonement, our only means [of atonement] is through repentance.[2] Repentance atones for all sins. Even if a person had been wicked all his life but repented [with absolute sincerity] at the very end, he is not called to account for any [previous] wickedness. The Day of Atonement, in itself, provides atonement for those who repent.[3]

4 The highest form of repentance is when one has resolved not to repeat the sin and indeed does not repeat it when later having the opportunity to do so. This demonstrates that the repentance was sincere and effective. If a person is not subsequently confronted with the same sin, the repentance is still valid. One should not seek temptation to test the strength of the repentance; it is preferable to stay out of temptation's way. However, if one happens to confront temptation successfully, this is a strong proof of the validity of the repentance.

5 The Talmud (*Taanit* 16a) quotes the opinion of Rabbi Adda bar Ahava: "One who sins and confesses but does not repent [in his heart], to what is this compared? To a person who holds a [dead] rodent in his hand; even if he immerses in all the seas of the world, the immersion is not valid. But if he casts [the rodent] from his hand, once he has immersed in [a mikvah] of forty measures [of water], the immersion is valid." Rabbi Adda's statement stresses the need not just for superficial ritual correctness, but for internal moral correctness. A person holding a dead rodent—which is an impure and defiling object—does not become pure merely by immersing in water, even if the immersion took place many times in the largest bodies of water. By holding the rodent, the person thereby demonstrates an ongoing direct connection with impurity, nullifying the effectiveness of the immersions. On the other hand, if a person casts aside the rodent, thereby removing the source of impurity, then he may immerse even in a small pool of water—the mikvah—and become purified.

The analogy to repentance is clear. One who holds the sin in hand but utters words of repentance remains defiled. It does not matter how elaborate the words of confession and regret; as long the sin is in hand, no atonement can be effected. However, if the person casts off the sin, then words of confession and repentance can purify.

Chapter Two

1. What is complete repentance? It is when a person is confronted with the same situation in which he had sinned, and he has the power to [commit the sin] but refrains from doing so because of his repentance—not from fear and not from physical weakness. If one repents only in old age, at a time when no longer having the strength to do the sin [that had previously been committed], this is a valid repentance and [the person is considered to be a] penitent, even though this is not the highest form of repentance.[4]

2. What is repentance? It is when a person abandons his sin and casts it from his mind, and decides not to repeat it. He regrets that he sinned. He calls God as witness that he will never return to this sin again. He must confess verbally and articulate those matters that he decided in his heart.

3. One who confesses but had not decided in his heart to abandon [his sinful ways] is compared to one who has immersed [in a ritual bath to become purified] while holding a dead rodent in his hand! The ritual immersion is of no effect until he casts away the rodent.[5]

6 | Sin does not just happen on its own. Rather, it emerges from a context, the result of negative moral traits such as anger, jealousy, and greed. Sin is influenced by peer pressure. It grows out of ignorance of or apathy about religious beliefs and practices. If a person wishes to repent, it is not enough simply to declare good intentions. One needs to alter the context in which sin has been allowed to emerge. To do this, the penitent must improve personal character traits, stay away from sinful people, and study religious teachings and texts conscientiously.

7 | At the root of repentance is a candid awareness of one's shortcomings. One feels that life has not been lived properly, that God's word has been neglected. Sin is the result of arrogant disregard for the teachings of religion. A penitent can restore wholeness to life by uprooting the pride and vanity that have created a separation between the self and God. By living modestly and humbly, the penitent demonstrates control over the ego—the very source of so many negative character traits.

4. Among the ways of repentance are to call out to God with tears and supplications; to give charity according to one's ability; to greatly distance oneself from the context of one's sin;[6] to change one's name, as if to say, "I am someone else, and not the same person who did those [sinful] deeds"; to change one's behavior to the good and upright path; and to move away from one's place [of residence] because exile atones for sin by causing one to be humiliated, modest, and meek.[7]

8 Many of the laws of Judaism are of a ritual, ceremonial nature. They are considered to be in the category "between humans and God." Included in this category are such laws as those relating to the observance of the Sabbath and festivals, dietary restrictions, and ritual purity. Violations of these laws would seem to have no impact on fellow human beings. Rather, they primarily reflect disregard for God's commandments.

9 Interpersonal sins include those deeds that cause damage to another person or to his or her property. God does not grant atonement for such sins unless and until the transgressor gains forgiveness from the victim of the sin. Interpersonal sins constitute a violation of God's laws, as well as a violation of basic ethical behavior.

10 Interpersonal sins include not only physical damage caused to others or to their property, but also emotional damage caused by gossip, slander, or verbal insult. While it is more difficult to quantify compensation due for emotional damage, such damage can often be more severe and painful than loss of property.

11 The burden of interpersonal sin is not eliminated by the death of the victim. To gain atonement, the perpetrator must pacify the soul of the deceased and make restitution to the heirs. The goal of atonement is to purify one's own soul from sin and to be innocent in the eyes of God and fellow human beings.

9. Repentance and the Day of Atonement only atone for sins between human beings and God;[8] but interpersonal sins[9] are never forgiven until a person has made restitution and appeased the one whom he wronged. Even if he has returned the [illegally gotten] property to the rightful owner, he still has to appease him and ask for his forgiveness. Even if he merely belittled a person with words, he must appease him and go to him until he is granted forgiveness.[10]

10. It is forbidden for a person to be cruel and to withhold forgiveness. Rather, one should be easy to pacify and difficult to anger. When a sinner asks forgiveness, one should grant it with a full heart and willing soul. Even if the other had sinned greatly against him and caused him much anguish, he should not take revenge or bear a grudge.

11. One who sinned against another, but the victim died before the sinner could ask forgiveness: the guilty party should bring ten people with him to the grave of the victim [of his wrongdoing]. In their presence, he should say, "I have sinned against the Lord God of Israel and against this person [buried here], and I did such and such to him." If he owed money, he must pay it to the [victim's] heirs. If there are no heirs, he must give the money to the court and confess his sin.[11]

12 It seems reasonable to expect that the righteous are rewarded and the wicked are punished according to their deeds. Yet, we do not always see this direct correlation in this world. On the contrary, we see righteous people who suffer and wicked people who prosper. While accounts will ultimately be settled in the world to come, the question of why divine justice does not seem to operate consistently in this world remains perplexing. Maimonides addresses this dilemma by reminding us that only God knows the true nature of our merits and sins. God alone can make the necessary calculations to determine rewards and punishments. Because of our limited knowledge and perspective, we cannot fathom God's ways; but we should trust that all His ways are righteous, true, and just.

In his discussion of divine providence (*Guide of the Perplexed* 3:51, p. 625), Maimonides indicates that God's providence is correlated to a person's spiritual connection with the Almighty. If a person apprehends God in the right way, "he is with God and God is with him." But if a person abandons God, he thereby becomes separated from Him and "he becomes in consequence of this a target for every evil that may happen to befall him." When one lives in contact with the "divine overflow," God's providence is more manifest. When one distances from God, God leaves the person to the vagaries of nature.

13 The shofar is an animal's horn that serves as a musical instrument. The Talmud relates that the shofar is fashioned from the horn of sheep, goat, mountain goat, antelope, or gazelle (*Rosh Hashanah* 27a). The generally favored source for a shofar, by custom, is a ram's horn. The Torah refers to *Yom Teruah,* a day of sounding the shofar, as the first day of the seventh month, that is, the first day of Tishri, which is Rosh Hashanah (Numbers 29:1). The Torah offers no explanation as to why the shofar is to be sounded on this day. Presumably, it was a call to the public to highlight the solemnity of the day. In ancient times, the shofar served as an alarm in times of emergency.

(continued on page 116)

Chapter Three

1.   Each person has merits and sins. One whose merits surpass his sins is righteous. One whose sins surpass his merits is wicked. If they are evenly balanced, he is an average person. So it is with countries. If its residents' merits are greater than their sins, it is a righteous [country]. If their sins are greater than their merits, it is a wicked [country]. And so it is for the entire world.

2.   These calculations are only made in the mind of God because He [alone] knows how to weigh merits against sins.[12]

3.   Anyone who regrets the commandments he fulfilled and wonders about [the value] of the merits he acquired, and says in his heart, "What did I benefit by doing them? I wish I had not done them," has lost all of them, and none of them is ever accounted to him.

4.   Even though the sounding of the shofar on Rosh Hashanah is a divine command [with no reason for it given in the Torah],[13] it has symbolic meaning. It is as though it calls out: "Awaken from your sleep, you sleepy ones! Arise from your slumber, you slumbering ones! Examine your deeds and return in repentance and remember your Creator! You who forget the truth due to temporal vanities and who err after emptiness and nonsense, search into your souls and improve your ways and your deeds! Let each person abandon his evil ways and bad thoughts!" A person should see himself all year long as though he is half meritorious and half guilty. If he commits one sin, he tilts himself and the entire world to the side of guilt and causes its destruction. If he fulfills one commandment, he tilts himself and the entire world to the side of merit, and he brings salvation and redemption to himself and the world. As it is said, "And the righteous one is the foundation of the world" (Proverbs 10:25).

(continued on page 117)

Rabbinic tradition has offered various reasons for the blowing of the shofar on Rosh Hashanah. When Abraham was spared from sacrificing his son Isaac, he noticed a ram caught in the thicket by its horns (Genesis 22:13) and sacrificed the ram instead of Isaac. Thus, the ram's horn became a reminder of Abraham's profound faith in God. The story of Abraham's binding of Isaac is the traditional Torah reading on the first day of Rosh Hashanah, underscoring the connection to the ram's horn blown on this holy day. The shofar, in recalling the ordeal of Abraham and Isaac, serves as a plea of the people of Israel to God to remember the piety of our ancestors and to have mercy on us, just as He spared Isaac's life on that occasion.

The sounding of the shofar also recalls the Revelation at Mount Sinai, which was accompanied by the sounds of the shofar (Exodus 19:16). Just as the Israelites trembled in awe at Sinai, so the shofar evokes awe in us as we stand before God on Rosh Hashanah, which is considered to be a day of judgment.

Jewish tradition teaches that the messianic era will be ushered in with the sounds of the shofar. The silent prayer recited as the central devotion of the thrice-daily prayers includes the plea to the Almighty that He "sound the great shofar of our redemption." Thus, hearing the shofar on Rosh Hashanah elicits hope for a brighter future and for the ultimate salvation of humankind in messianic times.

Maimonides chose to emphasize the shofar's role as a wake-up call, alerting us to the need for repentance. While not negating the earlier-cited rabbinic traditions, he tied the shofar's significance not to past or future events, but to the specific lives of each of us who hears the blasts of the ram's horn.

14 Many traditional Jewish communities observe the custom of reciting nightly or early morning supplicatory prayers, known as *Selihot*, beginning one month before Rosh Hashanah and continuing until the day before the Day of Atonement.

Therefore, it is customary among all the house of Israel to increase charitable giving, good deeds, and the performance of commandments during the period between Rosh Hashanah and the Day of Atonement more than at any other time of the year. They arise at night during these ten days to pray in their synagogues and to offer supplications and words of contrition until daybreak.[14]

15 In Maimonides's view, the ultimate punishment for egregious heretics and sinners is that their souls are cut off from life in the world to come (*Sanhedrin* 10:2). They simply cease to exist; their souls are deprived of the infinite bliss of being in the presence of God.

16 Yehoyakim (sometimes spelled Jehoiakim) ruled Judah from 609 to 598 BCE. His reign is described in 2 Kings 23 and 24, as well as in 2 Chronicles 36. In the early years of his reign, Judah was a vassal state of Egypt. In 605 BCE, Babylonia defeated Egypt in battle and seized control of Syria and the land of Israel. Yehoyakim complied with Babylonian rule for three years but then rebelled. He died an ignominious death in the ensuing onslaught by the Babylonians.

Rabbinic tradition portrayed Yehoyakim as a thoroughly wicked man, defying God and God's law in every possible way. He publicly violated the Torah and promoted idolatry. His shameful death was seen as a fitting punishment for his heretical and immoral life. Maimonides picks up on one rabbinic tradition that Yehoyakim, because of his public desecration of the Torah's laws, forfeited his place in the world to come.

6.   The following have no place in the world to come, but are cut off, destroyed, and judged eternally due to the gravity of their evils and sins;[15] apostates, heretics, deniers of the Torah, deniers of the resurrection of the dead and of the future coming of the Messiah, rebels, those who cause the public to sin, those who separate themselves from the life of the community, those who commit sins arrogantly and publicly like Yehoyakim,[16] informers, those who cast fear on the public when it is not for the sake of Heaven, murderers, gossipers, and men who make themselves appear as though they are not circumcised.

17 Rabbi Abraham ben David of Posquieres (ca. 1125–1198), who wrote a critical gloss on the *Mishneh Torah*, took strong issue with Maimonides for his branding as an apostate anyone who believed that God has corporeal attributes. "Why did he call such a one an apostate? Many who were greater and better than he followed this way of thinking." Rabbi Abraham pointed out that those who attributed corporeal features to God were led to this belief by texts in the Torah and rabbinic literature that described God in physical terms. While they had understood these texts in a philosophically incorrect manner, they should not be categorized as apostates because of their simplistic reading of the Bible and rabbinic homilies.

Maimonides, though, was adamant in his insistence on the absolute noncorporeality of God. He brooked no compromise on this position; if misguided people take literally the corporeal descriptions of God in the Bible and rabbinic literature, their error is inexcusable. They lose their portion in the world to come! Everyone needs to have enough philosophical training to know that God has no physical qualities.

7. Five are in the category of apostates: one who says there is no God and that the world has no Overseer; one who believes there is an Overseer but that there are two or more of them; one who believes there is One Master but that He is corporeal and has physical form;[17] one who believes He was not the primordial Being and Foundation of all; and one who worships a star or heavenly body, or something of the sort, believing it to be an intermediary between himself and the Master of the universe.

18 Maimonides bases this statement on a passage in the Talmud (*Sanhedrin* 99a) which refers to a verse in the Torah: "Because he has despised the word of the Lord, and has broken His commandment; that soul shall utterly be cut off, his iniquity shall be upon him" (Numbers 15:31). Who is meant by one who has despised the word of the Lord? The Talmud answers that it refers to someone who states the Torah is not from Heaven, even if the person claims merely that just one verse was composed by Moses on his own.

19 One of the great rabbinic figures of the early second century BCE was Antigonos of Sokho. Among his teachings was the statement: "Be not like servants who serve their master in order to receive a reward; but be like servants who serve their master not in order to receive a reward; and let the fear of Heaven be upon you" (*Pirkei Avot* 1:3). He was stressing the idea that religion should be observed for its own sake, not with the intent of reaping rewards. According to rabbinic tradition, two of Antigonos's students—Zadok and Boethus—misunderstood their rabbi's intent. They thought that Antigonos meant there was no ultimate reward or punishment, that is, no afterlife in the world to come. Zadok and Boethus broke away from their teacher and developed their own followings; their disciples became known as Sadducees and Boethusians, respectively. These schools rejected the authority of the Oral Torah, preferring to base themselves on a more literal reading of the Written Torah. They denied belief in an afterlife and in reward and punishment after death.

Rabbinic Judaism, the tradition to which Maimonides adheres, strenuously maintained the authenticity of the Oral Torah and the authoritative role of the sages in transmitting and interpreting it. The Boethusians and Sadducees were viewed as heretical sects that veered from the truth of Judaism, largely due to their rejection of the Oral Torah's authority. In the introduction to his commentary on the Mishnah, Maimonides provides a detailed account of the transmission of the Oral Torah, generation by generation from the time of Moses. He makes it clear that the Written Torah and the Oral Torah are inextricably linked together and that both are essential elements in Judaism.

8. Three are in the category of heretics: one who denies prophecy and believes that no information can be transmitted from God to human beings; one who denies the prophecy of Moses our teacher; and one who says that the Creator is unaware of human actions. Three are in the category of deniers of the Torah: one who believes that the Torah did not derive from God, or that a verse or word [did not derive from God] but that Moses composed it on his own;[18] one who denies the [authoritative] interpretations [of the Written Torah], that is, the Oral Torah, and contradicts its [authoritative] teachers as did Zadok and Boethus;[19] and one who says that God replaced a [Torah] commandment for another commandment, and that the Torah—even if it had originally been given by God—has been voided.

20 A person who sins through ignorance, convenience, or carelessness needs to repent but has not forfeited a place in the world to come. One who spitefully and publicly sins is in a different category; such a person demonstrates defiance of God's law and therefore loses a place in the world to come. An example of the first type of sinner is someone who eats forbidden food because it is less expensive or easier to obtain. The motive for the transgression is not rebellion against God, but a matter of personal convenience. Given equal access to permitted food, such a person would more than likely opt for the permitted food. An example of the second type is someone who eats forbidden food despite having equal access to permitted food. That person eats the forbidden food as a sign of rejection of the dietary laws, as though God did not command these laws. The sinner's motive is spiteful rebellion—and the punishment is commensurate.

21 Apostasy is the ultimate rejection of Torah. If a Jew is compelled to convert to another religion on pain of death, martyrdom is to be preferred to apostasy. If a Jew converted under duress, though, Maimonides himself ruled that he or she is not subject to punishment by human courts, nor is the soul cut off by the divine court, because the sin was committed through compulsion ("Foundations of the Torah" 5:4). The forced convert does not lose a place in the world to come as long as he or she maintains Jewish faith inwardly and strives to move to another land where Judaism can be practiced openly. In the present passage, Maimonides notes that if a forced convert subsequently adopts the new religion willingly and repudiates Judaism, the consequence is the loss of a place in the world to come.

9.   There are two types of rebels—one who rebels against a particular commandment, and one who rebels against the entire Torah. A rebel against a particular commandment has established himself as one who does this sin intentionally, is accustomed to it, and is publicly known to do it. This applies if he transgresses spitefully.[20] A rebel against the entire Torah is one who converts to another religion [even] at a time of religious oppression[21] and adheres to that religion, saying, "What is the value of clinging to the people of Israel who are lowly and oppressed? It is better for me to cling to these who have power."

22 If one sins, one may ultimately feel remorse and decide to repent. However, if one causes others to sin, the situation becomes much more complicated. How can a person fully repent who has coerced, misled, or lured a person to sin and does not know the full extent of the damage done? The victim has sinned and perhaps has then influenced family and friends to do likewise; these victims have influenced yet others. The one who started this wave of sins cannot possibly know all the individuals who were negatively impacted—and thus cannot find them to explain his errors and ask their forgiveness.

23 These cases refer to the sin of turning an innocent person over to ruthless people who will torture or murder or who will confiscate the victim's property unjustly. In places where there are honest and fair court systems, though, this ruling does not apply. All residents, whether Jewish or non-Jewish, must follow the laws of the land in which they live, assuming that the laws are just and are implemented fairly and impartially.

Throughout much of the past two thousand years—and even today in some lands—Jews were not granted equal rights and were not given fair treatment in non-Jewish courts. Indeed, until the modern period, Jewish communities generally operated their own rabbinic court system and handled all internal issues themselves. Occasionally an aggrieved Jewish person would turn to non-Jewish courts where bribes could be given and harsh punishments meted out. The Jewish community considered it a heinous crime for a Jew to turn over a fellow Jew for judgment in the non-Jewish courts, when the case should have been handled within the Jewish court system. Maimonides's description of "informers" relates to Jews who unscrupulously endanger the life or property of fellow Jews by turning them over to a corrupt court system or whose informing against fellow Jews could elicit a harsh retribution against the entire Jewish community.

10. Those who cause the public to sin—this refers to causing great sins or to causing light sins, even the violation of a single positive commandment. [This also refers to those] who force others to commit sins or who mislead or seduce others [into sin].**22**

11. One who separates himself from the life of the community—even if he did not transgress any sins—is one who stays separate from the congregation of Israel and does not fulfill commandments among them, and does not share their sufferings nor fast on their fast days. He acts as though he were a member of one of the [other] nations, as though he were not an Israelite: he has no place in the world to come. Those who commit sins arrogantly [thereby demonstrate that they] are not embarrassed to transgress the Torah.

12. Two are in the category of informers: (1) one who turns over an Israelite to an idolater to be murdered or beaten; (2) one who turns over an Israelite's property to an idolater or violent person.**23**

13. One who casts fear over the public not for the sake of Heaven is one who dominates the public forcefully so that they fear and dread him. [This refers to one whose] intention is [to bolster] his own honor, not for the glory of Heaven.

14. There are sins [seemingly] lighter than the [above mentioned sins] that our sages still regarded as causing one to lose his place in the world to come, if he were accustomed to them. It is proper to distance oneself from them and guard oneself from them. They are giving someone a nickname [that displeases him], calling someone by a [despised] nickname [that others have given him], embarrassing someone in public, deriving

(continued on page 129)

24 Parents must provide for the well-being of their children. This includes not only providing for the children's physical needs, but also tending to their emotional, educational, spiritual, and social needs. Among a parent's responsibilities, the Talmud (*Kiddushin* 29a) lists ensuring that a child (1) receives a proper education in Torah, (2) learns a trade (or suitable occupation) so that the child will become a responsible adult, (3) marries an appropriate mate, and (4) learns how to swim, that is, gains life-preserving skills. The goal of parents is to raise religious, self-sufficient, happy, and constructive children who will be able to take their places in the community when they grow into adulthood.

Parents must provide a home that fosters high ideals and moral behavior. Children growing up within a healthy environment will be more likely to develop healthy attitudes and practices. If a parent sees that a child is not behaving appropriately, the parent must provide the necessary guidance and encouragement to bring the child back to the acceptable path. A parent should not allow the child to persist in negative behavior patterns on the assumption that the child will self-correct with the passage of time. Parents who do not attempt to correct their children become accomplices in the child's future misdeeds. Parents who feel unable to handle a difficult child on their own should consult those with experience and expertise in dealing with problem children.

honor through the disgrace of another, despising rabbinic scholars, despising one's teachers, profaning [the sanctity] of festivals. When do these people forfeit their place in the world to come? This is only if they die without having repented. But if they repented from evil and died as penitents, then they have a place in the world to come; for nothing withstands [the power of] repentance. Even a person who denied the essence of faith all his life but repented at the end of life has a place in the world to come. All the sinners and rebels and similar such offenders—if they repented openly or secretly, they are received as penitents.

Chapter Four

1. Twenty-four things obstruct [one from doing] repentance. Four of them are great sins; if one does them, the Holy One, blessed be He, does not assist penitence due to the gravity of the sin: (1) one who causes the public to sin, including one who prevents the public from fulfilling a commandment; (2) one who influences another to follow the wrong [religious] path; (3) one who sees his child following bad ways but does not prevent [the child's descent into wickedness]. Since the child is in his domain, if he would have stopped the child, the child would have turned away [from evil]. It is as though the parent caused the child to sin [by failing to chastise the child];**24** included in this category is one who could have stopped others [from sin]—whether individuals or groups—but did not do so, and left them in their errors; (4) one who says, "I will sin and then later repent"; included in this is one who says, "I will sin and the Day of Atonement will absolve me of my sins."

25 People generally do not like to be chastised for their sins. If they recognize their errors and wish to repent, they will do so whether or not they receive chastisements from someone else. If they do not recognize their errors and do not wish to repent, they will not likely listen to critical words from an outsider. Yet, people need to receive responsible chastisement from time to time; otherwise, they grow complacent and do not feel impelled to improve their ways. Criticism, if properly and lovingly given, is an essential ingredient in one's spiritual growth.

Who, though, is able to give chastisement that will be accepted by the public? Maimonides offers several criteria for the ideal chastiser:

1. The person must be a great sage. The public must feel confident that the chastiser is a learned person who has the knowledge and wisdom to offer suitable advice. If a community is unable to obtain the services of such a sage, it should engage the most learned person available.

2. The person should be elderly. Jewish values inculcate respect and reverence for elders. People may not readily take criticism from their peers, let alone from someone younger than they are, but they will be more likely to defer to an elderly sage. If an elderly sage is not available, the community may engage a younger person, as long as this person commands the respect of the public. Indeed, it may happen that a younger sage will have greater credibility than an older person who is not as learned.

3. The person should be God-fearing from youth. If the chastiser has an impeccable reputation for piety, people are more likely to listen seriously. If the speaker has a spotty past, the public might think: Who is this person to chastise us, since his own past is filled with sins? However, if the best available chastiser has a blemished past, he nonetheless may be appointed.

4. The person must be beloved by the community. People must feel that the chastiser speaks with love, not anger; that he genuinely is concerned with their souls and is speaking from the heart. A sincere, beloved speaker is more effective than a flowery orator who is more interested in rhetoric than in the lives of the people.

2.   Five situations block the repentance process: (1) a person who separates himself from the community, because he will not be included among them nor share their merit when they repent; (2) one who disputes the words of the sages, because his contentiousness will separate him from the sages, so that he will not to know the ways of repentance; (3) one who mocks the commandments because they are debased in his eyes, so he will not pursue them or fulfill them; (4) one who despises his own teachers, because this causes him to alienate himself from them, so that he will have no one to teach him and guide him along the true path; and (5) one who despises chastisements, because he thereby closes himself off from repentance, since chastisements induce repentance. When a person is informed of and embarrassed by his sins [through chastisements] he will then turn in repentance. It is a responsibility of each Jewish community to engage a great and elderly sage,[25] God-fearing from his youth and beloved by the community, who will chastise the public and return them in repentance.

26 This case refers to a poor person who barely has enough food to feed the family. Out of embarrassment or feeling of social obligation, he invites someone to a meal, knowing full well that there is not enough food to feed the family and the guest. If the invitee knows that the invitation was extended as a social courtesy and that the poor person really does not have enough food to serve the guest, then the invitee should politely decline the invitation. If the invitee does accept the invitation, he should eat a minimal amount. If he eats from the poor person's meal while knowing that he thereby is depriving the poor person's family of food, then the invitee is guilty of something akin to theft. It is not outright theft, since the person has eaten with permission food that the host had offered. In halakhah, this is called *avak gazel*, the "dust" of theft.

3. In five cases, it is impossible to achieve complete repentance because [the person's actions] constitute sins against others who do not even know the sin was committed against them; thus, they are unable to offer forgiveness, nor is the sinner able to ask forgiveness: (1) one who curses the general public, and not just one specific person from whom he would have been able to ask forgiveness; (2) one who divides stolen goods with a thief and does not know the proper owner of the stolen goods [and therefore cannot make restitution]. The thief steals from many people; by dividing the stolen goods [with the thief] he thereby abets him and encourages him to sin more; (3) one who finds a lost object and does not attempt to return it to the owner. Later, when he decides to repent, he will not know to whom to return the object; (4) one who takes advantage of the poor, orphans, and widows. These are unfortunate people, not well known, who wander from city to city without anyone knowing who they are. [One who cheats them] will not know to whom to return the property; and (5) one who takes bribes to pervert justice; he does not know the full consequences of this [perversion of justice] or how much damage it did. I Ic will be unable to make restitution because he will not know all the victims who were affected by his injustice. Moreover, he abets the [briber] in his evil ways.

4. There are five categories [of transgressions] where it is presumed a person will not repent because they are considered light matters among most people, and the sinner will tend to rationalize that no sin was committed: (1) one who eats from a meal that is not sufficient for the host. This smacks of theft, but the person imagines he did not sin, saying that "I only ate with [the host's] permission",[26] (2) one who uses a poor person's

(continued on page 135)

27 This case deals with one who lends money to a poor person and takes a pledge as security. The pledge—which may be a simple tool, such as a shovel or plow—is to be held until the poor person repays the loan. The lender has no right to use the item pledged; however, a lender may think that there is no harm in doing so because they are not expensive items. Using these items causes them to wear out a bit and to depreciate in value; the lender, though, will not consider this slight damage to the pledge to be of significance and will not think of repaying the lost value to the borrower. Nor will the lender repent for this sin, not even realizing a sin was committed. Yet, the halakhah considers the lender to be guilty of theft. This is an example of how careful a person must be when dealing with the property of another.

pledge, such as a shovel or plow, rationalizing that he has not depreciated their value and has not stolen anything;**27** (3) a man who looks at [sexually arousing women], rationalizing that there is no sin in that because he did not have immoral physical contact. He does not realize ogling is a great sin that leads one to illicit physical contact; (4) one who derives honor through the shame of another, rationalizing that he did not sin directly and did not cause the other's shame. He only compared himself favorably so he would appear honorable and the other would appear disgraceful; and (5) one who casts suspicion on the innocent, rationalizing that he did not do anything to the other, having only raised a suspicion of which the person might or might not be guilty. He does not realize that it is sinful to cast suspicion of sin on an innocent person.

5. There are five things that when a person does them, he is likely to continue doing them; they are difficult to extricate from one's behavior patterns. A person must be careful not to cling to these very bad traits: (1) tale bearing, (2) gossiping, (3) being wrathful, (4) harboring evil intentions, and (5) maintaining friendship with a wicked person, because one will learn from and be influenced by the evil deeds [of the wicked person].

6. All of the above cited and similar such things serve to obstruct repentance, but they do not prevent it. If a person repented from them, he is [considered] a penitent and has a place in the world to come.

28 Maimonides inveighs against those who believe that human life is predetermined. At a time when many people gave credence to astrology, Maimonides staunchly opposed this pseudo-science because it taught that humans are governed by the position of stars and planets, and therefore lacked free will. In his *Letter on Astrology*, he faulted the ancient Israelites for turning to astrologers rather than recognizing their own responsibility to make reasonable decisions. He wrote: "That is why our kingdom was lost and our Temple was destroyed and why we were brought to this; for our fathers sinned and are no more.... They did not busy themselves with the art of war or with the conquest of lands, but imagined that these [astrological] studies would help them" (Isadore Twersky, *A Maimonides Reader*, p. 465).

Chapter Five

1. Free will is granted to every person. If one wishes, he can direct himself to the good path and be a righteous person. If he wishes, he can direct himself to the evil path and be a wicked person. Humanity is the unique species in the world [that is granted free will]; a human being has the capacity to know good and evil, to do what he wishes; one is not compelled to act one way or the other.

2. Do not pay attention to what the fools of the nations and the ignorant Jews say, for instance, that the Holy One, blessed be He, decrees upon a person from the moment of birth whether he is to be righteous or wicked. It is not so. Rather, each person can become as righteous as Moses our teacher or as wicked as Jeroboam, wise or foolish, compassionate or cruel, miserly or overly generous; likewise with all the traits. No one forces him or decrees his destiny or pulls him in one of these two directions. He himself willingly chooses the path he wishes to follow. Thus, if a person sins, he has diminished himself; therefore, it is fitting that he cry and weep over his sins and what evil he has done to his soul.**28**

3. The principle of [free will] is an essential and great foundation of Torah and the commandments. It is stated, "Behold, I have placed before you today life and good, and death and evil" (Deuteronomy 30:15). God does not compel a person nor decree that he do good or evil; rather, responsibility is given to humans to choose.

[29] Maimonides deals with an age-old dilemma. If God is all knowing, this means that He knows the future. If He knows the future, this implies that He knows everything every human being will ever do. If His knowledge is infallible, it would seem that humans are predetermined to act in the way already known by God. So how can we speak of free will?

In addressing this question, Maimonides suggests several approaches. First, we know that humans have free will through the Bible. God informed Moses and the prophets of this principle of life, and so we have God's own word testifying to its veracity.

Second, we can offer rational support to the biblical evidence. Since God is great enough to have created the laws of nature, He is also great enough to have created free will for human beings. Since He is endowed with Infinite wisdom, He is wise enough to know how to endow humans with free will.

[30] Reconciling God's omniscience and human free will is a dilemma that is ultimately not solvable. Human beings lack the ability to understand the full nature of God and God's knowledge. Since we cannot fathom how God "knows" things, we have no access to how He has endowed humans with free will. This is simply a given, as demonstrated by the Bible.

4.   If God had decreed that a person will be righteous or wicked; or if people were programmed from birth to think or act in a particular way, as foolish astrologers think, then how could He command us through the prophets to do this and not to do that, to improve ourselves and not to follow after our wicked ways? If from birth [our actions] had already been decreed, it would be impossible to veer from them. What would be the point of the entire Torah? How could a wicked person be subject to punishment or a righteous person to reward [if all their deeds were preordained and not performed through their own free will]? Will the Judge of all the earth not do justice?[29] [Just as God created the laws of nature] so He granted that human beings be autonomous and be responsible for their actions. Therefore, we are judged according to our deeds.

5.   We do not have the intellectual capacity to understand how the Holy One, blessed be He, knows all the creations and [their] actions.[30] But we do know without any doubt that the deeds of humans are in their own hands and that the Holy One, blessed be He, does not force or decree anyone to do anything. This is known not only from our religious tradition, but from clear proofs from the teachings of wisdom. Because this is so, it has been taught by [our] prophets that a person is judged according to his deeds, whether good or bad. This is a principle upon which all prophecy depends.

31 The prophet Isaiah said, "Peace, peace to the distant and to the near, said the Lord, and I will heal him" (Isaiah 57:19). The Talmud (*Berakhot* 34b) explains that the "distant" refers to one who had been far from God but who has now come close through repentance, while the "near" refers to one who had always remained close to God. The Talmud notes that God first greeted the one who had been distant, and only afterward the one who had always been close. The moral lesson is that God, in some way, appreciates the penitent even more than the purely righteous. The penitent had been accustomed to a life of sin and had to overcome old habits and beliefs; coming close to God was achieved only through struggle and sacrifice. In this respect, a perfectly righteous person cannot reach the level of the penitent, not having had to undergo the same struggles to overcome a sinful lifestyle.

Praising the spiritual accomplishments of penitents is a way of acknowledging them and of accepting them as worthy members of the religious community. Penitents may feel ashamed of their past lives and may not see themselves as being equal to those who have always been religious. The eloquent passages in rabbinic literature in praise of the virtues of penitents help alleviate those feelings of embarrassment, alienation, or self-deprecation.

Chapter Seven

1. Since humans are endowed with free will, each person should strive to repent and confess his sins and to wash his hands from sin so that he will die as a penitent and will merit the life of the world to come.

2. A person should constantly view himself as though he is about to die—and might die right now while still a sinner. Therefore, one should repent [sins] immediately and not say, "I will repent when I grow old," because maybe he will die before growing old. Solomon said in his wisdom, "At all times your clothing should be white" (Ecclesiastes 9:8).

3. Do not think that repentance only applies to sins that entail action, for example, adultery, robbery, and theft. Rather, just as one must repent from these, so one must scrutinize his evil traits and repent from anger, enmity, jealousy, mockery, greed for money and honor, gluttony, and so forth. These [latter] are more severe than sins that entail action; when a person is steeped in [these bad traits], it is difficult to break from them.

4. A penitent person, due to his past sins, should not consider himself to be distant from the status of the righteous. It is not so. Rather, he is beloved and endeared by the Creator, as though he had never sinned. Moreover, he has great merit because he had tasted sin and separated himself from it and overcame his [evil] inclination. Our sages taught that the perfectly righteous cannot reach the same level as a penitent.[31] That is to say, the [penitents'] level is higher than that of [the perfectly righteous] who have never sinned, because the [penitents] have overcome their [evil] inclinations more than the [perfectly righteous have had to do].

32 The Talmudic sage Rav, who lived in the third century CE, described the world to come as an existence where "there is neither eating nor drinking nor begetting children, neither bargaining nor jealousy nor hatred nor strife. All that the righteous do is to sit with their crowns on their heads and enjoy the radiance of the Divine Presence" (*Berakhot* 17a). This seems to have been the prevalent Jewish view during Talmudic times, and this is the view adopted by Maimonides.

5. All the prophets commanded repentance. Israel will not be redeemed except through repentance. The Torah has already assured us that Israel will ultimately repent at the end of their days of exile and will be immediately redeemed [at that time].

6. Great is repentance because it brings one near to the Divine Presence. Repentance brings near those who were distant. Yesterday [before repenting, the sinner] was despised, abominable, distant, and disgusting to God. Today [after repenting], he is beloved and cherished, near and a friend.

8. It is the way of penitents to be very meek and humble. If fools taunt them by [reminding them] of their earlier misdeeds, they should pay no attention to them; rather, they should hear [these taunts] and remain happy in the knowledge that this is a merit for them. Whenever they are embarrassed by and ashamed of their earlier deeds, their merit increases and their [spiritual] level grows. It is an outright sin to taunt a penitent by reminding him of past misdeeds.

Chapter Eight

1. The good hidden away for the righteous is the life of the world to come: life after which there is no death, good that is not intermingled with bad.**32** The reward of the righteous is that they will merit this pleasantness and dwell in this goodness. The punishment of the wicked is that they will not merit this [eternal] life but will be cut off and die forever.

2. In the world to come, there are no physical bodies. The incorporeal souls of the righteous exist like the ministering angels. There is no eating or drinking or anything else that human bodies need in the [earthly] world. [In the world to come, the souls of the righteous] understand and perceive elements of the truth of the Holy One, blessed be He, that they could not understand when they were in their coarse and lowly bodies.

33 Maimonides offers a more elaborate discussion of messianic times at the end of the *Mishneh Torah*, in chapter 12 of the "Laws of Kings and Wars." He writes that the laws of nature will continue to operate as usual. The difference between our times and messianic times is that in messianic times Israel will no longer be oppressed by the nations of the world; and all humanity will believe in the One God. The prophets and sages yearned for the days of the Messiah so that Israel would be free to devote itself to the Torah and its wisdom and thus be worthy of life in the world to come. Maimonides teaches that in messianic times, there will be no famine or war, no jealousy or strife. "Blessings will be abundant, comfort within the reach of everyone. The single preoccupation of the entire world will be to know the Lord." This will be a time of fulfillment of Isaiah's prophecy (Isaiah 11:9): "For the earth will be full of the knowledge of the Lord as the waters cover the sea."

Chapter Nine

1.   The Holy One, blessed be He, gave us the Torah, a tree of life.
     One who fulfills its words and understands them with a complete
     and correct understanding will merit the life of the world to
     come. One's merit is in proportion to the greatness of his deeds
     and abundance of his wisdom. The Torah assures us that if we
     fulfill [its teachings] with happiness and good-heartedness, and if
     we meditate on its words constantly, then God will remove from
     us those obstacles that [would prevent us from the fulfillment
     and study of Torah], such as illness, war, famine, and so forth. He
     will induce positive factors to strengthen us in fulfilling the Torah,
     such as abundance, peace, financial well-being, so we will not
     need to spend all our days attaining those things that the body
     needs. Rather, we will be able to have leisure to study wisdom and
     fulfill the commandments so as to merit life in the world to come.

2.   All Israel, their prophets and sages, have yearned for the days
     of the Messiah, to find rest [from the oppression] of the nations
     that do not allow them to properly devote themselves to
     Torah and the commandments. [During messianic times,
     Israel] will find serenity to increase wisdom and come to merit
     life in the world to come. In those days [of the Messiah],
     knowledge and wisdom and truth will increase. That king [the
     Messiah] will arise from the house of David, a person wiser
     than Solomon, a great prophet almost equal to Moses. He will
     teach all the Jewish people and guide them in the ways of
     God. All the nations will come to hear him. Messianic times
     will occur in this world, and nature will continue on its usual
     course. However, sovereignty will return to Israel. Our sages
     have taught that there is no difference between this world and
     messianic times, except [that in messianic times, Israel will not
     be] subjected to the rule of the nations.[33]

34 | The highest form of spirituality is achieved when a person feels a close relationship with the Almighty. Although God is infinitely transcendent, He is also infinitely imminent. Our forefather Abraham is described in the Torah as God's "friend," that is, a person who achieved a high level of closeness with God. This is a model to which we should aspire.

The Torah, as God's word, provides a means of deepening our "friendship" with God. The commandments are to be viewed not as externally imposed burdens but as God's invitation to enter into a closer relationship with Him. By fulfilling His instructions with love, we thereby demonstrate our "friendship" and come to feel a greater intimacy with Him.

Chapter Ten

1. A person should not say, "I will fulfill the Torah's commandments
   and engage in wisdom so that I will receive the blessings
   written [in the Torah] or so that I will merit life in the world to
   come." Nor should one say, "I will avoid committing the sins
   that the Torah forbade so that I will be spared from the curses
   recorded in the Torah, or so that I will not be cut off from life
   in the world to come." It is not appropriate to serve God in
   this way. One who does so serves from fear; this is not the
   level of prophets or sages. Only the ignorant serve God in this
   way, until their understanding increases and they come to
   serve God from love.

2. One who serves [God] from love is one who studies Torah and
   fulfills commandments and walks in the ways of wisdom not
   because of any ulterior motive—not because he fears
   punishment or wishes to reap reward. He performs the [right
   and] true because it is [right and] true. The good will result as
   a consequence. This is a high virtue that not every sage
   attains This was the virtue of Abraham our father, whom the
   Holy One, blessed be He, called "My friend" because he only
   served [God] from love. This is the virtue that the Holy One,
   blessed be He, commanded us through Moses, saying, "And
   you shall love the Lord your God" (Deuteronomy 6:5). When
   a person loves God with proper love, he will then observe the
   commandments with love.[34]

35 It is best to study Torah without ulterior motives, simply for the love of Torah and the love of God. Yet, if one has not yet attained such a lofty level, a person should still engage in Torah study even from the desire to gain rewards. It is hoped that the experience of Torah study will elevate the student, who will then gradually transition into the proper study of Torah for its own sake.

36 Maimonides concludes his *Book of Knowledge* with the same theme with which he opened it: the commandment to know God. Since love of God is correlated with knowledge of God, greater love leads to greater knowledge, and greater knowledge increases the level of love. Each person should exert his or her intellect to the extent possible to achieve this highest goal of humanity: to know God.

3. What is the proper love? It is when one loves God with an exceedingly great and overwhelming love; his soul is bound in love of God so that he is constantly thinking of God like one who is lovesick.

5. Anyone who studies Torah to receive reward or to fend off troubles is engaging in Torah not for its own sake. Anyone who studies Torah not from fear and not to gain reward, but only because of love of the Master of the world who commanded it, engages in Torah for its own sake. Our sages taught: let a person engage in Torah even not for its own sake, because ultimately he will come to engage in Torah for its own sake.[35] When teaching children and the ignorant, we stress punishments and rewards; but as their understanding and wisdom grow, we teach them, little by little, the ideal of engaging in Torah because of love. We convey this gently until they grasp and understand this secret [wisdom], and then they will serve God in love.

6. It is known and clear that one's love of the Holy One, blessed be He, is not rooted in his heart unless he meditates on it constantly and properly, until he abandons extraneous matters and focuses only on this. The Torah commands [that one must love God] "with all your heart and with all your soul" (Deuteronomy 6:5). One's love of God is in proportion to his knowledge of God. Therefore, a person should devote himself to understanding and contemplating those wisdoms and insights that give knowledge of the Creator, according to the capacity of a person to understand and comprehend.[36]

1 According to Maimonides, we have been given a theological and philosophical "problem": to exert our intellects to obtain knowledge of God. But we have also been given the correct answer by the Torah: God exists. Those who are intellectually gifted will work on the problem and arrive at the correct answer. Those who are less gifted will work on the problem, but may not arrive directly at the correct answer. They will then need to review their speculations and detect where they erred. Once they do this, they will be able to rethink the problem and come to the correct conclusion.

But what about those who struggle to obtain knowledge of God but do not come to the correct conclusion? One group may say: "Even though I am unable to know God through philosophical speculation, I accept that God exists. Even if I had some doubts about the veracity of the 'answer' while I was working on the problem and may still have some reservations, I accept that the answer is correct and will live my life on the assumption that God exists." Such people are not heretics. Although they have not "solved" the problem, and although they remain perplexed, they essentially accept that the "answer" given to them is correct. Such individuals have not forfeited their place in the world to come.

Another group, though, consists of those who did not arrive at the correct conclusion. In spite of their intellectual efforts, they did not achieve belief in / knowledge of God. But members of this group then conclude: "Since I have not arrived at the given answer, I deny that the answer is correct." It is only this latter group that Maimonides would brand as heretics.

2 See note 4 on page 4 in the commentary on "Laws of Foundations of the Torah."

☐ Thirteen Principles of Faith

1. To believe[1] in the existence of the Creator, may He be blessed; namely, that there is a Being who is complete in every manner of existence. He is the Cause of all that exists. He maintains their existence, and their existence is dependent on Him. Do not imagine the absence of His existence, because His absence would nullify all other existents and nothing could exist without His existence. If we were to imagine the absence of all other existents except for Him, the existence of the Name, may He be blessed, would not be annulled or diminished. For He is sufficient in His existence and is self-sustaining, not needing anything else to sustain Him. The existence of everything beside him—angels, heavenly spheres, and all that is within them and all that is below them—depends on Him. This first principle is taught in the phrase "I am the Lord your God" (Exodus 20.2) [2]

3 See note 5 on page 6 in the commentary on "Laws of Foundations of the Torah."

4 See note 17 on page 120 in the commentary on "Laws of Repentance."

Dr. Marc Shapiro cites numerous rabbinic authorities who disagreed with Maimonides's approach (*The Limits of Orthodox Theology*, chapter 3). Some believed in God's corporeality, basing themselves on the literal reading of biblical and rabbinic literature. Others accepted God's noncorporeality but rejected Maimonides's claim that corporealists lost their place in the world to come. They felt that God would not deprive such people from eternal life for holding a mistaken view, especially because this view was directly attributable to words in the Bible and rabbinic lore.

Maimonides was surely aware that many of his contemporary Jews—including those in the learned classes—held corporeal notions about God. He took on himself the responsibility of purging Judaism from this unsophisticated and incorrect way of thinking about God. He had no patience for simplistic pietists who clung to primitive theological ideas that were refuted by philosophy and reason. Since religion and reason can never be in conflict—both derive from the same Author of Truth—it is imperative to harmonize them whenever an apparent conflict arises.

I believe that Maimonides wrote strongly and dogmatically on this topic because he knew that many Jews did not share his views. I suggest that Maimonides used this threat as a rhetorical device, not as a literal theological truth. After all, he was wise enough to know that it was God—and not he—who determined who had a share in the world to come. Just as the Bible and rabbinic sages employed figurative language—so did Maimonides!

2. The Unity of God; namely, that we must believe that He who is the cause of all is One. [This "One"] is not like one of a pair, or one of a kind, or one person composed of many parts, and not one like one physical thing that can be divided and separated infinitely. Rather, He most high is One and a Unity unlike any other unity. This second principle is taught in the phrase "Hear O Israel, the Lord our God, the Lord is One" (Deuteronomy 6:4).**3**

3. The negation of corporeality; namely, that we must believe that this One is not a physical body and not a force in a body, and not subject to things that affect bodies, such as movement, rest, and dwelling.**4** Therefore, our sages of blessed memory negated [the possibility] of composition or separation [in God]. All passages in Holy Scriptures that describe Him in physical terms—for example, walking, standing, sitting, speaking, and so forth—are in metaphorical language. Our [sages] of blessed memory said: "The Torah speaks in the language of man" [*Berakhot* 31b]. This third principle is taught in the phrase "for you saw no manner of form on that day when the Lord spoke to you in Horeb" (Deuteronomy 4:15). That is, you did not perceive Him as having form because He—as we have stated—is not a body nor a physical force.

4. That God is Primordial; namely, that this One was the absolute First, and nothing existed before Him. This fourth principle is taught in the phrase "the Primordial God is a dwelling-place" (Deuteronomy 33:27).

5 | In Maimonides's view of pure religion, one should worship God directly, not through intermediaries of any kind. It is not only forbidden to worship idols or entities of nature, it is also prohibited to consider these things as objects that have power to intercede with God on one's behalf. Maimonides objected to belief in divine intermediaries because such belief can lead to idolatry itself, as happened in the days of Enosh (see "Laws of Idolatry" 1:1–2). Once supernatural powers are granted to things other than God, it is only a short jump to seeing those objects as godlike in and of themselves. Moreover, turning to intermediaries diminishes the spiritual stature of the individual; it implies that one is unworthy or unable to worship God directly, but needs to find indirect means of approaching God.

One also should not pray to angels or call on them to bring one's prayers to God. Each person has direct access to God. Maimonides, though, does seem to condone a prayer to angels in his "Laws of Prayer" 7:5. He records a Talmudic rule (*Berakhot* 60b) that one should utter a prayer before entering the privy. One should say: "Be honored you holy honorable ones, servants of the Most High. Protect me, protect me. Wait for me until I enter and come out, since this is the way of humans." This prayer seems to be directed to angels. Yet, in *Guide of the Perplexed* 3:22 (p. 490), Maimonides refers to the Talmudic notion that two angels accompany a person but interprets this to mean that each person is "accompanied" by a good inclination and an evil inclination—not by actual angels.

Maimonides's recording of the prayer before entering the privy may, indeed, indicate an exception to his overall view concerning angels and the prohibition of directing prayers to them. He may have conceded to the literal Talmudic tradition in this case, in deference to popular fears about entering the dirty and unholy precincts of the privies of those days.

Or, perhaps this passage, too, should be understood metaphorically, rather than literally. The "holy honorable ones" may refer to the good and evil inclinations. The words "protect me, protect me" may be directed to God, not to the good and evil inclinations. The request that they wait until the person comes back out of the privy may simply be a figurative indication that while one is in the privy, the moral and spiritual conflicts of the good and evil inclinations remain outside. While this is a stretched interpretation of Maimonides's text in Laws of Prayers, it fits in better with his general philosophical stance.

5. That God, blessed be He, is alone worthy of worship, adulation, exaltation, and obedience to His commandments. One must not worship any lesser beings—for example, angels, stars, heavenly spheres, the elements and anything made from them—because these all function by their natures without self-determination or free will; but [we must] only worship the Name, may He be blessed. It is not proper to worship those things as though they are intermediaries between humans and God; rather, one should direct his thoughts only to Him and put aside anything other than Him. This fifth principle is taught in the Torah's prohibitions of idolatry.[5]

6 Ten levels of angels emanate downward from the pure intellect of God. The lowest level of these angels is the intellectual link between God and His creations. Prophets rise to this level, referred to as the "active intellect" in philosophical terminology, where they receive divine messages.

We might understand Maimonides's view by means of an illustration drawn from the existence of radio waves. These waves are constant and ubiquitous, yet human beings do not hear messages from these waves unless they have a radio. The more powerful the radio, the more waves will be picked up. There are radios with antennae so powerful that they can pick up signals from across the world.

Likewise, God's spiritual "waves" are constant and ubiquitous. Yet, human beings do not hear these waves unless they tune in. The greater one's spiritual antennae, the greater one's reception of God's spirit. While the average person picks up little or nothing from God's constant and ubiquitous spirit, sages and philosophers are able to receive more of the divine influx. A prophet, who is at the pinnacle of human experience, has succeeded in developing spiritual antennae that receive more powerful and direct messages from God. Moses, as the greatest among prophets, had the most sensitive spiritual antennae.

Thus, prophecy does not represent any "change" in God: God is constant and ubiquitous. Rather, prophecy represents a change and development within the human being. Through piety, meditation, and philosophical analysis, the individual increases the power of his or her spiritual antennae so as to be able to receive God's word.

7 While other prophets received their visions through the intermediary of the active intellect or angel, Moses achieved an angelic status himself and spoke to God "face to face."

6.   That there is prophecy; namely, that one should know there are
      humans who are endowed with elevated and pure qualities and
      great perfection. Their minds have the capacity to receive pure
      intellectual form. Their human intellect then clings to the
      "active intellect"**6** and they draw from it a high inspiration: this
      is prophecy and this is its substance. To explain this principle in
      full would take much elaboration. It is not our intention to
      provide intellectual proofs for each of these thirteen principles,
      because this would entail a discussion of all the wisdoms. I am
      simply listing these principles in narrative form. There are many
      verses in the Torah that testify to the existence of prophecy.

7.   The prophecy of Moses our teacher; namely, that we must
      believe he is the father of all prophets who preceded or
      succeeded him. All prophets are of lesser status. He was chosen
      from among all humanity to attain an understanding of God
      beyond what any human being ever attained or ever will attain.
      His superiority to humans was such that he reached an angelic
      level and was included in the level of angels. There was no
      barrier between him and God that he did not penetrate. There
      was no physical obstacle [to his spiritual ascent], and he had no
      deficiencies great or small. In his [prophetic] understanding of
      God, the powers of imagination and sensation were annulled, as
      were the powers of desire and fantasy. Only his pure intellect
      remained. About this, it is said of him that he spoke with God
      without angelic intermediaries. The prophecy of Moses, peace
      be upon him, differed from the prophecy of other prophets in
      four respects: (1) The Name, blessed be He, only communicated
      with other prophets through an intermediary;**7** but with Moses,
      there was no intermediary. As it is stated, "face to face do I speak
      with him" (Numbers 12:8). (2) All other prophets received

(continued on page 159)

8 The Mishnah (*Sanhedrin* 10:1) teaches that one must believe that "the Torah is from Heaven" in order to have a share in the world to come. Maimonides interprets this phrase in a very literal sense: one must believe that each letter of the Torah was written by Moses at God's behest and that the Torah text we have today is identical with the Torah text given to Moses.

Yet, rabbinic tradition itself includes various views on the nature of the Torah text. Although the sages universally agreed that God inspired and sanctioned the Torah text, differences of opinion exist about important details. Scholars such as Abraham Joshua Heschel and Marc Shapiro have pointed to authoritative rabbinic traditions that held that Joshua wrote the last eight verses of the Torah; that Moses composed the book of Deuteronomy with divine inspiration, but not at the dictation of God; or that King David deleted parts of the Torah and put them into the book of Psalms instead. One might believe that the Torah is from Heaven but was given in segments at different times (see *Gittin* 60a). Indeed, the phrase seems to demand a general allegiance to the divine inspiration of the Torah, rather than the specific and narrow formulation presented by Maimonides.

Shapiro (*Limits of Orthodox Theology*, p. 120) has suggested plausibly that Maimonides's insistence that the Jewish masses affirm that the Torah text in their hands was entirely free from any textual corruptions, even to the last detail, stemmed from the widespread Muslim claim that the Jews had falsified the biblical texts. Even though this claim was patently absurd, Maimonides did not want to open any discussion on the integrity of the biblical text and did not want to generate doubts in the minds of the unsophisticated masses. This would mean that although Maimonides himself knew a broader range of options existed for understanding "Torah from Heaven," he chose the narrow interpretation to keep things uncomplicated for the common folk.

prophecy in their sleep, after a slumber overcame them so that their senses would be incapacitated and only pure thought remain. But Moses received prophecy during the day, whenever God appointed him. As God stated, "If there be a prophet among you, I the Lord make Myself known to him in a vision, I speak with him in a dream. My servant Moses is not so; he is trusted in all My house; with him do I speak mouth to mouth, manifestly and not in dark speeches. He beholds the similitude of the Lord" (Numbers 12:6–8). (3) When other prophets received prophecy, even in a vision and even through an intermediary, their powers weakened and their bodies crumpled; they were overcome with a great fear almost to the point of death. But Moses, peace be on him, was not like this. When God spoke with him, he was not overcome by fear or trembling at all. This was due to his intellectual clinging to God. (4) Other prophets could not receive prophecy at will, but only at God's will. Indeed, a prophet might go days or years without receiving a prophecy. But Moses, peace be on him, could prophesy whenever he wanted.

8.   Torah is from Heaven; namely, we must believe that the Torah we currently have and that we received through Moses our teacher is entirely from God. The Torah reached Moses from God, may He be blessed, in what the Torah describes metaphorically as "speech." Only Moses understood how the Torah was conveyed to him by God. He was like a scribe, copying down the history, stories, and commandments [as God instructed him].[8] There is no difference [in sanctity] between [seemingly unimportant details recorded in the Torah] and [the seemingly very important teachings in the Torah]. All the words of Torah derive from God. The Torah of God is perfect,

(continued on page 161)

9 | In the introduction to his commentary on the Mishnah, Maimonides writes: "Know that each commandment that the Holy One, blessed be He, gave to Moses our teacher, peace upon him, He gave together with its explanation." The explanations were given orally so that Moses would know the full intent of the written text of the Torah and thus be able to teach the Israelites how to properly fulfill the commandments. These oral explanations have the same weight of authority as the Written Torah. Indeed, the Written Torah cannot be fully understood without the explanations provided by the Oral Torah.[1]

pure, holy, and true. If someone should say that Moses wrote verses or stories on his own, our sages considered him to be a denier and one who interprets the Torah in a manner worse than all the heretics; such a person thinks that the Torah has a core and a chaff, and that the history and stories have no value and were composed by Moses. This is what is meant by the phrase "the Torah is not from Heaven." Our sages taught that one who believes the entire Torah is from God with the exception of one verse composed by Moses has disgraced the word of God. Each statement of the Torah contains wisdoms and wonders to one who understands them; one cannot fathom the full depth of its wisdom. This applies also to the Oral Torah, which likewise derives from God. That which we do today [in fulfillment of the prescriptions of the Oral Torah] is exactly what the Name, may He be blessed, conveyed to Moses. Examples of this are the laws relating to the form of the sukkah, *lulav*, shofar, tzitzit, tefillin, and so forth.[9] Moses was faithful in conveying these laws. The verse that teaches this eighth principle is "And Moses said: In this way you will understand that God sent me to do all these things, and that I have not done them from my own heart" (Numbers 16:28).

10 This principle teaches the eternal validity of the Written Torah and the Oral Torah. The Torah was given by God and is not subject to revision or abrogation.

Although the laws of the Torah are incumbent specifically upon the people of Israel, the Torah contains a code of universal morality for all humanity. Jewish tradition refers to this universal code as the Noahide laws, that is, the laws given to the children of Noah—in other words, all human beings. The Talmud (*Sanhedrin* 56a) discusses these laws, which include the prohibitions against blaspheming God, engaging in idolatry, murdering, stealing, committing sexual immorality, and eating the flesh taken from a living animal; and the positive commandment to set up a system for the administration of justice. Maimonides, in the "Laws of Kings" 8:11, states that a non-Jew who accepts these seven commandments and observes them carefully—recognizing that these commandments were given by God through the agency of Moses—is to be considered a "righteous gentile" and will have a portion in the world to come.

In the "Laws of the Sabbatical and Jubilee Years" 13:13, Maimonides makes clear that "every single individual from among the world's inhabitants" has access to God and to the ultimate life in the world to come. If anyone—Jewish or non-Jewish—strives to know God and to live wisely and piously, then "behold, this person has been totally consecrated, and God will be his portion and inheritance forever and ever."

9.   The authenticity of the Torah; namely, that the Torah of Moses was transcribed from the Creator, may He be blessed, and not from anyone else. One may not add nor subtract from either the Written Torah or the Oral Torah.[10]

10.   That God most High knows the deeds of human beings and does not turn His attention from them.

11 Although the ideal is to serve God without thought of reward or punishment, the masses find it difficult to reach this level of spiritual perfection. Thus, the Bible and our rabbinic sages inform the public that God does grant rewards to the righteous and does punish the wicked. In formulating this principle, Maimonides indicates that the ultimate reward is for one's soul to enjoy the presence of God in the world to come; the ultimate punishment is to have one's soul cut off and be deprived of dwelling in the presence of God in the world to come.

Rewards and punishments need to be understood not as specific actions taken by God, but as consequences of human behavior. For example, let us imagine two students taking a class in computer sciences. One student pays close attention to the teacher, takes notes, reviews the lessons, and practices regularly on the computer. The other student daydreams during class, does not take notes, does not review the work, and does not practice on the computer. At the end of the course, the teacher gives an exam to the two students. The attentive student receives an A, and the slothful student receives an F. Were these grades rewards and punishments from the teacher? No. They were grades that reflected the students' work or lack thereof. The A student was not "rewarded" with a good grade and was not "rewarded" with knowledge to use the computer; rather, this student earned these things through personal exertion. The F student was not "punished" with a bad grade and was not "punished" with ignorance of how to use the computer; rather, these were consequences of that student's own behavior.

So it is in the spiritual world of "rewards" and "punishments." The righteous person who learns Torah, who meditates on God, who engages in philosophical speculation about the nature of God, and who piously observes the commandments is "rewarded" with spiritual bliss in the world to come. This blessing is, in fact, a consequence of the attitudes and behaviors adopted during his or her lifetime. On the other hand, a person who does not study Torah, does not meditate on God, does not engage in philosophical speculation about the nature of God, and does

(continued on page 166)

11. That God most High gives reward to one who fulfills the commandments of the Torah and punishes those who transgress its prohibitions.[11] The ultimate reward is the world to come; the ultimate punishment is excision [of one's soul].

not observe the commandments with piety is "punished" by not obtaining the spiritual bliss in the world to come that he or she did not earn.

The blessings of the world to come should be seen as a consequence of one's life of piety and wisdom, not as an externally granted "reward." Likewise, if one has not lived a spiritual and righteous life, the natural consequence (not "punishment") is for the soul to be cut off.

12 This principle teaches that the messianic idea does not simply refer to a peaceful era, but entails the presence of a specific personality who will be descended from King David through the line of his son Solomon. Maimonides's insistence that the Messiah will descend through the line of Solomon may have been influenced by a passage in 1 Chronicles 28:5: "Of all my sons—for many are the sons the Lord gave me—He chose my son Solomon to sit on the throne of the kingdom of the Lord over Israel." In this verse, King David indicates that Solomon was specifically chosen by God to take David's place as king; this was not simply a human decision of David's. That Solomon's rule is sanctioned by God Himself is an indication that the messianic line of David will pass through the line of Solomon.

12. Messianic days; namely, to believe and trust that [the Messiah] will come soon. "And if he tarries—wait for him" (Habakkuk 2:3). One should not set a time nor try to calculate from biblical verses the date of his arrival. One must believe that he will have superior rank and honor to any other king that ever ruled. One should exalt and love and pray for him, according to what all the prophets from Moses to Malachi had prophesied. This principle entails belief that every king of Israel [including the Messiah] must be from the house of David and from the line of Solomon. Anyone who questions [the right of] this family [to kingship] thereby denies the Name, may He be blessed, and the words of His prophets.[12]

13　In Maimonides's view, the ultimate fulfillment of a human being is in the world to come, where one's soul dwells blissfully in the presence of God. If so, why would a soul want to be resurrected into its body? This would seem to be a demotion from the perfect bliss of the world to come.

Even in his own time, scholars questioned whether Maimonides actually believed in a physical resurrection of the dead. He never discusses this topic in his *Guide of the Perplexed*. Rabbi Abraham ben David, in his glosses on the *Mishneh Torah*, comments on "Laws of Repentance" 8:2: "The words of this man seem to me to be similar to one who says that there is no resurrection for bodies, but only for souls." Maimonides wrote an *Essay on Resurrection* to reassure the public that he indeed subscribed to the principle of physical resurrection. Yet, even after the publication of this essay, critics were not entirely convinced.

The belief in resurrection has a long history in Judaism, and Maimonides was well aware of this. Indeed, the *Amidah* (silent devotion), recited three times daily as the main prayer of each service, mentions in its second blessing that God resurrects the dead. Various biblical passages allude to the notion of resurrection: "I slay and revive; I wounded and I will heal" (Deuteronomy 32:39) and "God slays and revives; He brings down to Sheol and raises up" (1 Samuel 2:6), for example. The book of Daniel makes clear reference to resurrection (12:2–3): "And many of those who sleep in the dusty earth shall awake, some to everlasting life, others to everlasting reproach and contempt."

The Mishnah (*Sanhedrin* 10:1) specifically excludes from the world to come anyone who denies that the Torah teaches the principle of resurrection of the dead. Rabbinic literature is amply clear in describing this concept as referring to corporeal resurrection of the dead.

Given the history of the idea, it would have been difficult—if not impossible—for Maimonides to have openly denied or even spiritualized the resurrection. How would he have reconciled the idea of resurrection with his idea of the perfection of the world to come?

Here is a possible explanation, which I learned from a discussion with Professor Menachem Kellner of the University of Haifa. Maimonides

(continued on page 170)

13. Resurrection of the dead[13] [namely, that the righteous will be resurrected—only the righteous, not the wicked].

When a person believes in all these principles and his faith in them is clarified, he is included among "Israel"; it is a commandment to love him and have mercy on him, and to behave toward him as the Name, may He be blessed, commanded one to love and befriend his neighbor. Even if one sinned through surrender to evil inclinations, he is punished according to his sins, and yet he has a place in the world to come. He is considered an Israelite sinner. But if a person fails to believe in any one of these principles, he has removed himself from the community [of believers] and has denied the foundation [of our faith].

(continued on page 171)

believed that life in this world provides the opportunity for spiritual growth through both the acquisition of wisdom and the performance of God's commandments. Our place in the world to come correlates to how high a level of perfection our souls have attained in this world. Resurrection of the dead, therefore, gives a righteous soul an opportunity to return to the world in bodily form so that the person can reach even higher levels of wisdom and fulfillment of the commandments. When the resurrected person again dies at a later time, the soul will reach an even higher place in the world to come. Thus, the resurrection serves to increase a soul's ultimate satisfaction in the world to come. This is why Maimonides specifies that the resurrection is for the righteous, not for the wicked. The souls of the wicked have already been cut off.

14 Maimonides indicates that one must believe all of the Thirteen Principles of Faith or else be considered a heretic who has no place in the world to come. This is a very sharp, uncompromising position.

To understand Maimonides's intention in compiling the Thirteen Principles of Faith, I think we need to understand his general attitude relating to religious and philosophical truth. We have already seen that he believed that religion and philosophy could not be in ultimate conflict given that both derive from the same Source. If there seems to be a conflict between the two, then either we have not understood the religious teaching properly, or we have not done our science correctly. When we perceive a conflict between religion and reason, we need to find a way of reconciling them.

A dramatic example of Maimonides's methodology is his dealing with corporeal descriptions of God in the Bible. Since corporeality is a philosophically unsound position, Maimonides reinterprets all biblical texts that reflect God's corporeality. These texts must necessarily be understood metaphorically, as poetic figures of speech. He applies this same methodology when dealing with rabbinic passages that seem to be philosophically and rationally unacceptable. He calls for an interpretation of these passages in such a way as to bring them in line with reason.

(continued on page 172)

He is known as an atheist, a heretic, and one who "cuts among the plantings."[14]

I have elaborated on these matters because I thought them to be an aid to faith. Therefore, know them and succeed with them; review them many times. Contemplate them with a fine contemplation. If your heart should deceive you into thinking you have understood them at one or even after ten readings, the Name, may He be blessed, knows that your heart has led you astray. Do not rush when you read them; I did not put them together casually, but only after much thought and contemplation.

Let us apply this methodology to the expression "loses one's place in the world to come." Is this a phrase that is meant to be taken literally? Or is it an example of figurative, symbolic language?

In "Laws of Repentance" 3:6, Maimonides lists various categories of heretics and scoffers who have no place in the world to come. Later on (3:14), he lists other sins about which the sages taught that transgressors had no place in the world to come. Examples of this are giving a person or calling a person by an embarrassing nickname, shaming someone in public, and deriving honor from the shame of others. Should we really believe that the sages deprived a soul from a place in the world to come because the person called someone by an unpleasant nickname or caused embarrassment to someone? Or, should we rather interpret the rabbis' words in a figurative way, that is, these are serious transgressions worthy of severe punishment? It seems to me that the phrase "loses one's place in the world to come" needs to be understood figuratively, not literally.

Indeed, how would the sages or Maimonides know for sure who is or is not entitled to a portion in the world to come? This is something that only God can know and decide upon. All the sages or Maimonides can do is offer strongly emotional expressions of what they believe to be serious transgressions worthy of eternal punishment.

Thus, when Maimonides writes that those who deny any of the Thirteen Principles of Faith lose their portions in the world to come, he is writing figuratively, homiletically, even hyperbolically. He is not providing a philosophical position, because what he says cannot be proven philosophically. He is not providing a universally accepted prophetic or rabbinic tradition, since what he says is challenged in many details by many great and pious sages.

In presenting the Thirteen Principles of Faith, Maimonides delineates those central teachings of Judaism that he thought the Jewish public needed to believe. To underscore the importance of these principles, he used the strongly figurative, emotive language to the effect that if one fails to believe in these principles, one's portion in the world to come has been forfeited.

Notes □

1. Peter Berger and H. Kellner, *The Homeless Mind* (New York: Random House, 1973); see also Berger's book *The Heretical Imperative* (Garden City: Anchor Press, Doubleday, 1979).

2. Viktor Frankl, *Man's Search for Meaning,* (New York: Washington Square Press, 1984).

3. Isaiah Berlin, "Two Concepts of Liberty," in *The Proper Study of Mankind: An Anthology of Essays* (New York: Farrar, Straus and Giroux, 1997), 191–242.

4. Erich Fromm, *The Sane Society* (Greenwich: Fawcett Publications, 1970), 62f.

5. Joseph B. Soloveitchik, "The Lonely Man of Faith," *Tradition* 7, no. 2 (1965): 5–67. This essay has been published in book form, *The Lonely Man of Faith* (New York: Doubleday, 1992).

6. Marvin Fox, *Interpreting Maimonides* (Chicago: University of Chicago Press, 1990), 24.

7. Isadore Twersky, ed., *A Maimonides Reader* (Springfield, NJ: Behrman House, 1972), 407.

8. Ibid., 383.

9. Quotations in this paragraph are from Maimonides's *Essay on Resurrection,* as published in Abraham Halkin and David Hartman, *Crisis and Leadership: Epistles of Maimonides* (Philadelphia: Jewish Publication Society, 1985), 223.

10. Ibid., 319.

11. Yeshaiahu Leibowitz, *The Faith of Maimonides* (New York: Adama Books, 1987), 11.

12. Ibid., 16.

13. Menachem Kellner, *Maimonides' Confrontation with Mysticism* (Oxford: Littman Library of Jewish Civilization, 2006), chapter 7.

14. Isadore Twersky, *A Maimonides Reader,* 363.

15. Marvin Fox, *Interpreting Maimonides,* 329.

16. See Menachem Kellner's discussion in his book *Maimonides on Judaism and the Jewish People* (Albany: State University of New York Press, 1991), 75–76.

17. Isadore Twersky, *A Maimonides Reader,* 475–76.

18. Ibid., 454.

19. Ibid., 465.

20. Ibid., 472.

21. See Marc Shapiro, "Maimonidean Halakhah and Superstition," in his book *Studies in Maimonides and His Interpreters* (Scranton and London: University of Scranton Press, 2008), 95–150.

22. Abraham Halkin and David Hartman, *Crisis and Leadership: Epistles of Maimonides*, 33.

Thirteen Principles of Faith

1. Maimonides outlines five categories that are generally included within the framework of the Oral Torah. The first two relate specifically to the explanations God gave Moses along with the Written Torah: explanations that are alluded to in the Torah text and that can be derived by logical principles of interpretation; and laws received by Moses at Mount Sinai that are not alluded to in the Torah and that cannot be derived by logical principles of interpretation. Examples of the first category are that "eye for an eye" (Deuteronomy 19:21) means financial compensation for damages, and not literal extraction of an eye; and that "fruit of a beautiful tree" (Leviticus 23:40) refers specifically to an *etrog* (citron), and not to any other fruit. Examples of the second category are that the Torah must be written on parchment and with black ink and that the boxes of tefillin should be cubical, with the corners squared off. The teachings of these two categories have been accepted as authoritative and passed down from generation to generation. There are no controversies concerning these matters.

    Three other categories fall under the rubric of the Oral Torah, according to Maimonides. Although these categories reflect laws and interpretations that do not go back to the time of Moses, they nonetheless are to be considered as normative rules. The first concerns laws derived by our sages by means of logical interpretation of the Torah's text. Because different sages interpreted verses differently, controversies arose as to the proper ruling. The sages took a vote on the disputed issues and then ruled according to the majority opinion. In the Laws of Rebels (1:1), Maimonides notes that the Great Assembly of sages in ancient Jerusalem served as the foundation of the Oral Torah. They promulgated rulings based on majority vote, and these rulings became binding on all Israelites. This category of Oral Torah is by far the most extensive and is also the one in which rabbinic debate and controversy are widespread. The second category is laws promulgated by the prophets and sages in order to safeguard the observance of the Torah's commandments. These ordinances become binding on all Israel once they have been universally accepted. Maimonides cites the example of the rabbinic prohibition of cooking, eating, or deriving benefit from a mixture of fowl and milk. The Torah's laws prohibit mixing milk with the meat of kosher domesticated four-legged animals; to safeguard these laws, the rabbis extended the prohibition to mixing milk with the meat of fowl. Their concern was that people would become confused and not understand why meat and milk is forbidden but chicken and milk is allowed. In its early stages, this ordinance was not universally accepted. Rabbi Yosi Haglili permitted the mixture of milk and fowl, and the people of his town in northern Israel followed his ruling. However, after Rabbi Yosi's passing, the prohibition was universally accepted by all the Jewish communities, and this ordinance thus gained the status of an authoritative and binding law. It has the same weight of authority as other laws in the Oral Torah. The final category concerns rules and customs that were instituted for the public benefit; once established by the prophets or sages, these practices became binding on the Jewish people. Some of these rules relate to ritual practice (for instance, Moses instituted the rule that one must study the laws of each holy day in advance of its arrival); and some relate to financial matters (for example, Hillel instituted the *prozbul*, a system whereby debts are not cancelled during the sabbatical year.)

Selected Bibliography □

Angel, Marc D. *Maimonides, Spinoza and Us: Toward an Intellectually Vibrant Judaism*. Woodstock, VT: Jewish Lights Publishing, 2009.

Drazin, Israel. *Maimonides: The Exceptional Mind*. New York: Gefen Publishing Company, 2008.

Fox, Marvin. *Interpreting Maimonides*. Chicago: University of Chicago Press, 1990.

Halkin, Abraham, and David Hartman. *Crisis and Leadership: Epistles of Maimonides*. Philadelphia: Jewish Publication Society, 1985.

Hartman, David. *Maimonides, Torah and Philosophic Quest*. Philadelphia: Jewish Publication Society, 1976.

Kellner, Menachem. *Maimonides' Confrontation with Mysticism*. Oxford: Littman Library of Jewish Civilization, 2006.

———. *Maimonides on Judaism and the Jewish People*. Albany: State University of New York Press, 1991,

———. *Must a Jew Believe Anything?* London: Littman Library of Jewish Civilization, 2008.

———. *Science in the Bet Midrash: Studies in Maimonides*. Brighton, UK: Academic Studies Press, 2009.

Kraemer, Joel L. *Maimonides: The Life and World of One of Civilization's Greatest Minds*. New York: Doubleday, 2008.

Leibowitz, Yeshaiahu. *The Faith of Maimonides*. New York: Adama Books, 1987.

Maimonides, Moses. *Guide of the Perplexed*. Translated by Shlomo Pines. Chicago: University of Chicago Press, 1964.

Rosner, Fred. *Maimonides: Introduction to His Commentary on the Mishnah*. Northvale, NJ: Jason Aronson, 1995.

Seeskin, Kenneth. *Maimonides: A Guide for Today's Perplexed*. West Orange, NJ: Behrman House, 1991.

Shapiro, Marc. *The Limits of Orthodox Theology*. Oxford: Littman Library of Jewish Civilization, 2004.

———. *Studies in Maimonides and His Interpreters*. Scranton, PA: University of Scranton Press, 2008.

Touger, Eliyahu. *Hilkhot Yesodei haTorah.* Jerusalem: Moznaim, 1989. (Hebrew text and English translation)

————, and Za'ev Abramson. *Hilkhot De'ot,* and Eliyahu Touger, *Hilkhot Talmud Torah.* Jerusalem: Moznaim, 1989. (Hebrew text and English translation.)

————. *Hilkhot Avodat Kokhavim.* Jerusalem: Moznaim, 1990. (Hebrew text and English translation.)

————. *Hilkhot Teshuvah.* Jerusalem: Moznaim, 1990. (Hebrew text and English translation.)

————. *Pirkei Avot.* Jerusalem: Moznaim, 1994. (This volume includes the Hebrew text and English translation of the Thirteen Principles of Faith.)

Twersky, Isadore. *Introduction to the Code of Maimonides.* New Haven: Yale University Press, 1980.

————, ed. *A Maimonides Reader.* Springfield, NJ: Behrman House, 1972.

Weiss, Raymond L., and Charles Butterworth. *Ethical Writings of Maimonides.* New York: Dover Publications, 1975.

Bible Study / Midrash

Passing Life's Tests: Spiritual Reflections on the Trial of Abraham, the Binding of Isaac *By Rabbi Bradley Shavit Artson, DHL*
Invites us to use this powerful tale as a tool for our own soul wrestling, to confront our existential sacrifices and enable us to face—and surmount—life's tests.
6 x 9, 176 pp, Quality PB, 978-1-58023-631-7 **$18.99**

The Messiah and the Jews: Three Thousand Years of Tradition, Belief and Hope *By Rabbi Elaine Rose Glickman; Foreword by Rabbi Neil Gillman, PhD; Preface by Rabbi Judith Z. Abrams, PhD*
Explores and explains an astonishing range of primary and secondary sources, infusing them with new meaning for the modern reader.
6 x 9, 192 pp, Quality PB, 978-1-58023-690-4 **$16.99**

Speaking Torah: Spiritual Teachings from around the Maggid's Table—in Two Volumes *By Arthur Green, with Ebn Leader, Ariel Evan Mayse and Or N. Rose*
The most powerful Hasidic teachings made accessible—from some of the world's preeminent authorities on Jewish thought and spirituality.
Volume 1—6 x 9, 512 pp, Hardcover, 978-1-58023-668-3 **$34.99**
Volume 2—6 x 9, 448 pp, Hardcover, 978-1-58023-694-2 **$34.99**

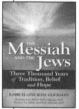

Masking and Unmasking Ourselves: Interpreting Biblical Texts on Clothing & Identity *By Dr. Norman J. Cohen*
Presents ten Bible stories that involve clothing in an essential way, as a means of learning about the text, its characters and their interactions.
6 x 9, 240 pp, HC, 978-1-58023-461-0 **$24.99**

The Genesis of Leadership: What the Bible Teaches Us about Vision, Values and Leading Change *By Rabbi Nathan Laufer; Foreword by Senator Joseph I. Lieberman*
6 x 9, 288 pp, Quality PB, 978-1-58023-352-1 **$18.99**

Hineini in Our Lives: Learning How to Respond to Others through 14 Biblical Texts and Personal Stories *By Rabbi Norman J. Cohen, PhD* 6 x 9, 240 pp, Quality PB, 978-1-58023-274-6 **$16.99**

The Modern Men's Torah Commentary: New Insights from Jewish Men on the 54 Weekly Torah Portions *Edited by Rabbi Jeffrey K. Salkin*
6 x 9, 368 pp, HC, 978-1-58023-395-8 **$24.99**

Moses and the Journey to Leadership: Timeless Lessons of Effective Management from the Bible and Today's Leaders *By Rabbi Norman J. Cohen, PhD*
6 x 9, 240 pp, Quality PB, 978-1-58023-351-4 **$18.99**; HC, 978-1-58023-227-2 **$21.99**

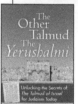

The Other Talmud—The *Yerushalmi*: Unlocking the Secrets of *The Talmud of Israel* for Judaism Today *By Rabbi Judith Z. Abrams, PhD*
6 x 9, 256 pp, HC, 978-1-58023-463-4 **$24.99**

Sage Tales: Wisdom and Wonder from the Rabbis of the Talmud
By Rabbi Burton L. Visotzky 6 x 9, 256 pp, HC, 978-1-58023-456-6 **$24.99**

The Torah Revolution: Fourteen Truths That Changed the World
By Rabbi Reuven Hammer, PhD 6 x 9, 240 pp, HC, 978-1-58023-457-3 **$24.99**

The Wisdom of Judaism: An Introduction to the Values of the Talmud
By Rabbi Dov Peretz Elkins 6 x 9, 192 pp, Quality PB, 978-1-58023-327-9 **$16.99**

Or phone, fax, mail or e-mail to: **JEWISH LIGHTS Publishing**
An imprint of Turner Publishing Company
4507 Charlotte Avenue • Suite 100 • Nashville, TN 37209
Tel: (615) 255-2665 • www.jewishlights.com
Prices subject to change.

Spirituality / Prayer

Davening: A Guide to Meaningful Jewish Prayer
By Rabbi Zalman Schachter-Shalomi with Joel Segel; Foreword by Rabbi Lawrence Kushner
A fresh approach to prayer for all who wish to appreciate the power of prayer's poetry, song and ritual, and to join the age-old conversation that Jews have had with God. 6 x 9, 240 pp, Quality PB, 978-1-58023-627-0 **$18.99**

Jewish Men Pray: Words of Yearning, Praise, Petition, Gratitude and Wonder from Traditional and Contemporary Sources
Edited by Rabbi Kerry M. Olitzky and Stuart M. Matlins; Foreword by Rabbi Bradley Shavit Artson, DHL
A celebration of Jewish men's voices in prayer—to strengthen, heal, comfort, and inspire—from the ancient world up to our own day.
5 x 7¼, 400 pp, HC, 978-1-58023-628-7 **$19.99**

Making Prayer Real: Leading Jewish Spiritual Voices on Why Prayer Is Difficult and What to Do about It *By Rabbi Mike Comins* 6 x 9, 320 pp, Quality PB, 978-1-58023-417-7 **$18.99**

Witnesses to the One: The Spiritual History of the *Sh'ma*
By Rabbi Joseph B. Meszler; Foreword by Rabbi Elyse Goldstein
6 x 9, 176 pp, Quality PB, 978-1-58023-400-9 **$16.99**; HC, 978-1-58023-309-5 **$19.99**

My People's Prayer Book Series: Traditional Prayers, Modern Commentaries *Edited by Rabbi Lawrence A. Hoffman, PhD*
Provides diverse and exciting commentary to the traditional liturgy. Will help you find new wisdom in Jewish prayer, and bring liturgy into your life. Each book includes Hebrew text, modern translations and commentaries from all perspectives of the Jewish world.

Vol. 1—The *Sh'ma* and Its Blessings
  7 x 10, 168 pp, HC, 978-1-879045-79-8 **$29.99**
Vol. 2—The *Amidah* 7 x 10, 240 pp, HC, 978-1-879045-80-4 **$24.95**
Vol. 3—*P'sukei D'zimrah* (Morning Psalms)
  7 x 10, 240 pp, HC, 978-1-879045-81-1 **$29.99**
Vol. 4—*Seder K'riat Hatorah* (The Torah Service)
  7 x 10, 264 pp, HC, 978-1-879045-93-0 **$23.99**
Vol. 5—*Birkhot Hashachar* (Morning Blessings)
  7 x 10, 240 pp, HC, 978-1-879045-83-5 **$24.95**
Vol. 6—*Tachanun* and Concluding Prayers
  7 x 10, 240 pp, HC, 978-1-879045-84-2 **$24.95**
Vol. 7—*Shabbat at Home* 7 x 10, 240 pp, HC, 978-1-879045-85-9 **$24.95**
Vol. 8—*Kabbalat Shabbat* (Welcoming Shabbat in the Synagogue)
  7 x 10, 240 pp, HC, 978-1-58023-121-3 **$24.99**
Vol. 9—Welcoming the Night: *Minchah* and *Ma'ariv* (Afternoon and
  Evening Prayer) 7 x 10, 272 pp, HC, 978-1-58023-262-3 **$24.99**
Vol. 10—Shabbat Morning: *Shacharit* and *Musaf* (Morning and
  Additional Services) 7 x 10, 240 pp, HC, 978-1-58023-240-1 **$29.99**

Spirituality / Lawrence Kushner

I'm God; You're Not: Observations on Organized Religion & Other Disguises of the Ego
  6 x 9, 256 pp, Quality PB, 978-1-58023-513-6 **$18.99**; HC, 978-1-58023-441-2 **$21.99**

The Book of Letters: A Mystical Hebrew Alphabet
  Popular HC Edition, 6 x 9, 80 pp, 2-color text, 978-1-879045-00-2 **$24.95**
  Collector's Limited Edition, 9 x 12, 80 pp, gold-foil-embossed pages, w/ limited-edition silkscreened print, 978-1-879045-04-0 **$349.00**

The Book of Miracles: A Young Person's Guide to Jewish Spiritual Awareness
  6 x 9, 96 pp, 2-color illus., HC, 978-1-879045-78-1 **$16.95** *For ages 9–13*

God Was in This Place & I, i Did Not Know: Finding Self, Spirituality and Ultimate Meaning 6 x 9, 192 pp, Quality PB, 978-1-879045-33-0 **$16.95**

Honey from the Rock: An Introduction to Jewish Mysticism
  6 x 9, 176 pp, Quality PB, 978-1-58023-073-5 **$16.95**

Invisible Lines of Connection: Sacred Stories of the Ordinary
  5½ x 8½, 160 pp, Quality PB, 978-1-879045-98-9 **$16.99**

The Way Into Jewish Mystical Tradition
  6 x 9, 224 pp, Quality PB, 978-1-58023-200-5 **$18.99**; HC, 978-1-58023-029-2 **$21.95**

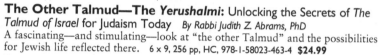

Theology / Philosophy

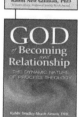

Believing and Its Tensions: A Personal Conversation about God, Torah, Suffering and Death in Jewish Thought
By Rabbi Neil Gillman, PhD
Explores the changing nature of belief and the complexities of reconciling the intellectual, emotional and moral questions of Gillman's own searching mind and soul.
5½ x 8½, 144 pp, HC, 978-1-58023-669-0 **$19.99**

God of Becoming and Relationship: The Dynamic Nature of Process Theology *By Rabbi Bradley Shavit Artson, DHL*
Explains how Process Theology breaks us free from the strictures of ancient Greek and medieval European philosophy, allowing us to see all creation as related patterns of energy through which we connect to everything.
6 x 9, 208 pp, HC, 978-1-58023-713-0 **$24.99**

The Other Talmud—The *Yerushalmi*: Unlocking the Secrets of *The Talmud of Israel* for Judaism Today *By Rabbi Judith Z. Abrams, PhD*
A fascinating—and stimulating—look at "the other Talmud" and the possibilities for Jewish life reflected there. 6 x 9, 256 pp, HC, 978-1-58023-463-4 **$24.99**

The Way of Man: According to Hasidic Teaching
By Martin Buber; New Translation and Introduction by Rabbi Bernard H. Mehlman and Dr. Gabriel E. Padawer; Foreword by Paul Mendes-Flohr
An accessible and engaging new translation of Buber's classic work—*available as an e-book only.* E-book, 978-1-58023-601-0 Digital List Price **$14.99**

The Death of Death: Resurrection and Immortality in Jewish Thought
By Rabbi Neil Gillman, PhD 6 x 9, 336 pp, Quality PB, 978-1-58023-081-0 **$18.95**

Doing Jewish Theology: God, Torah & Israel in Modern Judaism *By Rabbi Neil Gillman, PhD*
6 x 9, 304 pp, Quality PB, 978-1-58023-439-9 **$18.99**; HC, 978-1-58023-322-4 **$24.99**

From Defender to Critic: The Search for a New Jewish Self
By Dr. David Hartman 6 x 9, 336 pp, HC, 978-1-58023-515-0 **$35.00**

The God Who Hates Lies: Confronting & Rethinking Jewish Tradition
By Dr. David Hartman with Charlie Buckholtz 6 x 9, 208 pp, HC, 978-1-58023-455-9 **$24.99**

A Heart of Many Rooms: Celebrating the Many Voices within Judaism
By Dr. David Hartman 6 x 9, 352 pp, Quality PB, 978-1-58023-156-5 **$19.95**

Jewish Theology in Our Time: A New Generation Explores the Foundations and Future of Jewish Belief *Edited by Rabbi Elliot J. Cosgrove, PhD; Foreword by Rabbi David J. Wolpe; Preface by Rabbi Carole B. Balin, PhD* 6 x 9, 240 pp, Quality PB, 978-1-58023-630-1, **$19.99**; HC, 978-1-58023-413-9 **$24.99**

Maimonides—Essential Teachings on Jewish Faith & Ethics: The Book of Knowledge & the Thirteen Principles of Faith—Annotated & Explained
Translation and Annotation by Rabbi Marc D. Angel, PhD
5½ x 8½, 224 pp, Quality PB Original, 978-1-59473-311-6 **$18.99***

Maimonides, Spinoza and Us: Toward an Intellectually Vibrant Judaism
By Rabbi Marc D. Angel, PhD 6 x 9, 224 pp, HC, 978-1-58023-411-5 **$24.99**

Our Religious Brains: What Cognitive Science Reveals about Belief, Morality, Community and Our Relationship with God
By Rabbi Ralph D. Mecklenburger; Foreword by Dr. Howard Kelfer; Preface by Dr. Neil Gillman
6 x 9, 224 pp, HC, 978-1-58023-508-2 **$24.99**

Your Word Is Fire: The Hasidic Masters on Contemplative Prayer
Edited and translated by Rabbi Arthur Green, PhD, and Barry W. Holtz
6 x 9, 160 pp, Quality PB, 978-1-879045-25-5 **$16.99**

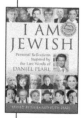

I Am Jewish
Personal Reflections Inspired by the Last Words of Daniel Pearl
Almost 150 Jews—both famous and not—from all walks of life, from all around the world, write about many aspects of their Judaism.
Edited by Judea and Ruth Pearl 6 x 9, 304 pp, Deluxe PB w/ flaps, 978-1-58023-259-3 **$19.99**
Download a free copy of the *I Am Jewish Teacher's Guide* at www.jewishlights.com.

*A book from SkyLight Paths, Jewish Lights' sister imprint

About SKYLIGHT PATHS Publishing

SkyLight Paths Publishing is creating a place where people of different spiritual traditions come together for challenge and inspiration, a place where we can help each other understand the mystery that lies at the heart of our existence.

Through spirituality, our religious beliefs are increasingly becoming a part of our lives—rather than *apart* from our lives. While many of us may be more interested than ever in spiritual growth, we may be less firmly planted in traditional religion. Yet, we do want to deepen our relationship to the sacred, to learn from our own as well as from other faith traditions, and to practice in new ways.

SkyLight Paths sees both believers and seekers as a community that increasingly transcends traditional boundaries of religion and denomination—people wanting to learn from each other, *walking together, finding the way.*

For your information and convenience, at the back of this book we have provided a list of other SkyLight Paths books you might find interesting and useful. They cover the following subjects:

Buddhism / Zen	Global Spiritual	Monasticism
Catholicism	Perspectives	Mysticism
Children's Books	Gnosticism	Poetry
Christianity	Hinduism /	Prayer
Comparative	Vedanta	Religious Etiquette
Religion	Inspiration	Retirement
Current Events	Islam / Sufism	Spiritual Biography
Earth-Based	Judaism	Spiritual Direction
Spirituality	Kabbalah	Spirituality
Enneagram	Meditation	Women's Interest
	Midrash Fiction	Worship

Or phone, fax, mail or e-mail to: SKYLIGHT PATHS Publishing
An imprint of Turner Publishing Company
4507 Charlotte Avenue • Suite 100 • Nashville, TN 37209
Tel: (615) 255-2665 • www.jewishlights.com
Prices subject to change.

For more information about each book, visit our website at www.skylightpaths.com